RELIABLE TRUTH

Also by Richard E. Simmons III

The True Measure of a Man
Safe Passage
Remembering the Forgotten God

THE VALIDITY OF THE BIBLE
IN AN AGE OF SKEPTICISM

RELIABLE
TRUTH

RICHARD E. SIMMONS III

Union Hill
Publishing

Union Hill is the book publishing imprint of The Center for Executive Leadership, a 501(c)3 nonprofit organization.

www.TheCenterBham.org

ISBN 978-1-939358-00-4

PRINTED IN THE UNITED STATES OF AMERICA

0 1 2 3 4 5 6 7 8 9

Dedicated to three of the great treasures

in my life, my children, Dixon, Dorothy Pate, and Will.

TABLE OF CONTENTS

PREFACE

RELIABLE TRUTH

Over the years, I have had numerous conversations with people about God, religion, and belief. One observation I feel comfortable in making is that all people have some opinion about God. Everyone has their own personal belief system, even if it is atheism. But regardless of who I am speaking with, I always like to ask a final question: How did you come to these conclusions in your spiritual life?

I often wonder how many people actually ask themselves why they believe what they believe. In fact, I would say it is not only appropriate but also right to give *considerable* thought to where we get our ideas about God, even if we are skeptical that he even exists. What has shaped and formed our views of spiritual reality? What are the primary sources that have formed our spiritual ideas and beliefs? Most significantly, how reliable are these sources?

I think most of us today, in a culture flooded with information at every turn, will, over the course of time, take this information and seek to forge a coherent, rational belief. For me, personally—and this goes back over thirty years—I had reached a point where I deeply desired to know why I should believe the Bible is God's word. I wanted to know what evidence existed that could prove the biblical story is in harmony with secular history. This became increasingly important to me because, although I saw that the Bible had the ring of truth, I felt a need to rationally justify more about why I believe it is the word of God.

Others, however, may believe the Bible is nothing more than an ancient book of myths and legends, or they may simply not really be sure of what it is, or they may just not care. Regardless, they, too, in fact, need to exercise their intellectual integrity and try to come to an understanding of how and why they believe as they do. How did they come to *that* conclusion?

Whenever you have a belief system or put your faith in something, that belief or faith must have a rational foundation, one that is grounded in reality.

IN THE MANNER OF PAUL

There have been a multitude of sources that have influenced and ultimately shaped my views and ideas about God and the spiritual world. As I look back, in my early years, I was not looking for a belief in God. That belief just kind of formed as I grew up, and I never questioned its validity because it came from people I trusted with my very life, particularly my parents. Honestly, my faith and its foundations was never really important to me as a young man.

It was not until college that I began to question my beliefs. I began to wonder if all the sources that had influenced and ultimately shaped my spiritual views were reliable. I began to wonder if my beliefs were true. I came to a point in my life where I realized that the primary source for what I believed about God and spiritual reality was the Bible. How could this ancient book, albeit a book that has been and remains revered by so many, *actually* be the divine word of God?

This led me on my search to understand why so many people over the centuries have indeed believed it to be the ultimate source of spiritual truth. At the time, I found the Bible to be experientially true; however, I needed more than that. I desired a solid, intellectual foundation for my spiritual life. I recognized that I needed a faith that I could believe in my head as well as in my heart. I was looking for good reasons to believe the Bible was the true word of God.

This book tracks a series of presentations I gave over the course of the last year. You will readily see that my style of delivery is to turn to the world's leading scholars, experts, and commentators on the subjects that touch on the Bible's legitimacy. Thus, in my efforts to communicate truth and wisdom to others in my talks, I have fashioned my style after the apostle Paul when he delivered his famous speech in Athens to the pagan Greek thinkers and intellectuals (Acts 17). In order to connect with them, Paul quoted from their poets and philosophers that they might better understand the spiritual truth he was trying to convey. This book, therefore, lays out the conclusions I have come to while standing on the shoulders of many giants of scholarship.

Richard Earl Simmons III
October 25, 2012
Birmingham, Alabama

ONE

WHEREVER TRUTH MAY LEAD

There are issues on which it is impossible to be neutral. These issues strike right down to the roots of man's existence. And while it is right that we should examine the evidence, and make sure that we have all the evidence, it is equally right that we ourselves should be accessible to the evidence. We cannot live a full life without knowing exactly where we stand regarding these fundamental issues of life and destiny.

– Sir Hector Hetherington
Principal of Glasgow University
(1936-1961)

C. S. LEWIS

C. S. Lewis is among the most influential Christian writers of the twentieth century.

Many people are somewhat surprised to learn that Lewis, who was dutifully raised in a traditional Christian household in Ireland, actually became an avowed atheist in his early teens while attending public school at the prestigious Malvern College in England. It would be years later, after World War I and well into his years at Oxford University, before he began his great search for a deeper and richer understanding of God's existence.

Lewis writes that there were two events in his life that ultimately led him to the Christian faith. The first step began when he read G.K. Chesterton's book, *Everlasting Man*, and the second, he has written, had a "shattering impact" on him. This event occurred one night, when one of the more militant atheists on the Oxford faculty staff, a man by the name of T.D. Weldon, came to his room and confided that he believed the historical authenticity of the Gospels appeared to be surprisingly sound.

This conversation deeply disturbed Lewis. He reasoned that if such a staunch atheist as Weldon thinks the Gospels may be true, where does that leave him? Lewis, you see, had always believed the New Testament stories to be nothing more than mere myths; there wasn't a shred of history or practical truth in them.

He began to reason that if the Gospel stories are in fact true, then this would mean all other truth would have to fade into insignificance. For the first time, he says, he began to wonder if his whole life was headed in the wrong direction.

Weldon's remarks about the historical authenticity of the Gospels wouldn't let him rest, as the conversation echoed in his memory and continued to haunt him. So Lewis, a determined seeker of truth, began an investigation. He decided to carefully read the entire New Testament in the original Greek. And as he read through the text, he was surprised at what he found.

Lewis, a professor of English literature at Oxford, had spent his entire professional life studying ancient manuscripts. And though, up to that time, he had never seriously read the Bible, he nonetheless considered it to be one of the world's great myths, like Norse mythology. The Gospels, Lewis noted, didn't contain the rich, imaginative writing techniques of most ancient writings. With a literary critic's ear for language and meter, Lewis recognized that the New Testament didn't contain the stylized and carefully-groomed qualities one would expect in any myth-making culture.[1]

Lewis writes, the Gospels,

> . . . appeared to be simple, eye-witness accounts of historical events primarily by Jews who were clearly unfamiliar with the great myths of the pagan world around them . . . I was by now too experienced in literary criticism to regard the Gospels as myth. They had not the mythological taste.[2]

Lewis continues, emphasizing that the Gospels were different from anything else he had ever read in ancient literature,

> Now as a literary historian, I am perfectly convinced, that whatever else the Gospels are, they are not legends. I have read a great deal of legends and myth and am quite clear that they are not the same sort of thing. They are not artistic enough to be legends. From an imaginative point of view,

they are clumsy; they don't work. Most of the life of Jesus is totally unknown to us and no people building up a legend would allow that to be so.[3]

And so, as an expert in ancient documents and languages, he began to wonder, If these aren't myths and legends, then what are they? Were they truly eyewitness accounts of historical events that actually took place?

Here we have this brilliant man, C.S. Lewis, an expert in ancient literature, a man of integrity and great education, who for so many years had dismissed the Gospels—the most influential body of writing in the Western world—simply because they sounded so unconvincing and without merit.

Everything changed, however, when Weldon, his trusted friend and colleague, an atheist with absolutely no trace of bias or hidden agendas, admitted that he found it highly likely that the Gospels present historically accurate accounts of the life of this man Jesus.

ANNE RICE

Anne Rice began her career as an immensely popular writer of vampire novels and holds the somewhat dubious claim to fame of having reintroduced and revitalized the vampire in modern culture. Her book *Interview with a Vampire,* made into a movie with Tom Cruise and Brad Pitt, made her a wealthy woman. She has written several vampire novels and much of her early writing life had been dedicated to this genre.

Rice, who was raised in the church, lost her faith during her college years. After college, she married an atheist and began writing novels in the 1970s. But then, fast forward to 1998, when she shocked the literary world and her many fans by announcing that she had returned to the Christian faith of her childhood.

In the steps leading to her return, Rice set out to research the life of Jesus. She began her personal search for biblical truth with the contemporary writings of eminent Christian scholars and theologians known as the so-called "Jesus scholars," many of whom had participated in a highly publicized series of academic conferences in the mid-1980s. Eventually, most of these scholars would publish their findings, a large number of them refuting the divinity of Jesus altogether.

Rice had taken her own, independent path to discover the truth of the biblical narratives. Having read much of the academic literature, she was stunned at what she found, expressing amazement at just how weak the scholarship seemed to be coming out of these high-profile Jesus seminars,

> Some books were no more than assumptions piled on assumptions. Conclusions were reached on the basis of little or no data at all. The whole case for the non-divine Jesus who stumbled into Jerusalem and somehow got crucified, that whole picture which had floated around the liberal circles that I frequented as an atheist for thirty years, that case was not made . . . Not only was it not made, I discovered in this field some of the worst and most biased scholarship I had ever read.[4]

Rice then applied her considerable talents to even further study of the Bible and theology, and, eventually, just as Lewis had, she reached the conclusion that the Gospels were historically accurate and, in fact, true. In short order, by 2002, she not only committed herself to Christ, she had also decided to use her writer's instincts and judgments to write her own fictional interpretation of the life of Jesus. She would present Jesus not as a mere man but as truly divine, "consecrating her writing entirely to Christ, vowing to write for him or about him."

Rice would eventually publish her first work on the life of Jesus, *Out of Egypt*, in 2005, close to a year after the publication of *The Da Vinci Code* by Dan Brown, a highly controversial bestselling suspense novel based on the premise that Jesus had been married and had had children and that his descendants are living to this very day. Rice, in direct opposition to the premise of *The Da Vinci Code*, is quick to point out that although her work is strictly fiction (and should be taken as such), it is firmly rooted in historical scholarship. Unlike Dan Brown, who creates a fanciful historical thriller with absolutely no dispositive historical documentation, Rice takes the position that Jesus is indeed who the biblical record says he is.

And so, here we have two truth seekers, C. S. Lewis and Anne Rice, two examples of individuals who came to believe in the Christian faith based solely on the fact that they had concluded the Gospels to be historically accurate and true. However, each of them took the time, with a conscious open-mindedness, to examine the evidence. It becomes quite clear that they did not embrace the teachings of Jesus *until* they were convinced that the source of the message was true. Once they had determined that the teachings were true, based solely on the evidence, they realized the necessity of living their lives in harmony with that truth.

The bottom line is that if you don't believe Christianity to be true, you're forced to believe the stories in the Bible are nothing more than myths and legends. However, if they can be demonstrated to be historically accurate where does that leave you? The questions of historical accuracy or inaccuracy haunted C. S. Lewis and troubled Anne Rice. Both of them were driven by their emotions and their intellects on their own, unique spiritual quest. Both turned to the Bible and, when they did so, they both realized that the Bible and everything in it pointed to the truth.

A GOOD PLACE TO START

For centuries, Christians have held the belief that the Bible (both the Old and New Testaments) is God's chief means of communicating his thoughts to mankind. It is the primary way he has made himself known. Jesus confirms this when he continually quotes the Old Testament by first saying, *"It is written,"* and then following with the verses quoted from the text. The Bible is considered a book of revelation in that it reveals to mankind spiritual truths that we would otherwise never know. This is why the Russian author Fyodor Dostoevsky said,

> My faith is not built on arguments of logic or reason, it is built on one thing—revelation.[5]

Within the Old and New Testaments, what do we find? We find poetry; we find divine laws and principles for living; we find a detailed and well-preserved record of Jewish history—the lives of the prophets, the Psalms, the life of Jesus, and the life of the early Church. And it's clear that this written revelation exists to be taught and passed on to every succeeding generation.

Nevertheless, the question that always seems to come up in our culture, and it plagues the skeptical mind, How do we know that this book is truly God's written revelation?

As C.S. Lewis began his search, one of the things that troubled him was wondering about the relevance of the Gospel story to modern life, to modern people. It's a legitimate question. How can such an ancient document, passed down over the millennia, have any relevance in an age of machines, the internet, and extraordinary conveniences? Lewis was puzzled,

What I could not understand was how the life and death of someone else two thousand years ago could help us here and now.[6]

It seems logical that the nature of a personal God is to speak. A loving God, a personal God would desire to communicate his thoughts and his presence to his creation. To be known. To love and to be loved. Self-expression is inherent to who he is. He is a personal, relational God.

Christianity teaches that God is speaking to the world, continuously articulating his words and his will to mankind. He is saying, seek me and you will find me. If that's true, many people will never find him, because they fail to seek or look. Only those who are willing to seek will find. Only those whose hearts are set on finding the truth will find it.

You would think this is what everyone in life would desire—to hear the voice of God. Seek me and you will find me. Seek me and you will hear my voice. And if a man or a woman truly desires to seek God (and C. S. Lewis and Anne Rice are certainly good examples), it seems the Bible would be a great place to start.

THE FOUNDATION OF KNOWLEDGE

Truth should be our exclusive aim in forming our beliefs. In fact, there are often serious consequences when we develop false beliefs about reality. French philosopher Blaise Pascal wrote that one of the primary reasons we struggle so much in life is a result of the false beliefs we develop.

Christians believe that faith and reason do not conflict, but instead complement one another. Reason does not and cannot cause a true faith, but reason can and will, when properly applied, support faith. St. Augustine, considered by many to be one of the great Christian thinkers of the early Church, defined "faith," as "trust in a reliable source," and, as such, he showed that it is an indispensable element of knowledge. We cannot live without faith, and Augustine recognized that it is imperative that the source in which we put our faith be reliable and true.[7]

A good example of our need for reliable sources can be found in the Bernie Madoff scandal, probably the greatest Ponzi scheme ever.

Now that the dust has settled (with his son Peter just recently pleading guilty), many new insights have come to light. A great deal of reporting on the financial details and on the innocent parties involved provides sobering perspectives on just how such a betrayal could have happened on such a massive and truly unprecedented scale.

What stands out most clearly, however, is that Madoff's fraud was made possible because so many people simply trusted him. Countless intelligent men and women, we learn, confessed to having invested large amounts of money because of the reputations of the noteworthy and famous individuals who were long-time investors in Madoff. The entire foundation of trust was based on very little, if any, first-hand information.

The message we learn from the Madoff scandal is that it is all too easy to believe almost anything when we place excessive trust in what people tell us. In the memorable words of President Ronald Reagan, when dealing with all other leaders of the world, the president's responsibility to the American people is to "trust, but verify."

When I was a young boy, I was told to believe the Bible. As I grew older, I was told to accept it as the written revelation of God by several trusted and influential people. However, I was never given a good reason why I should believe it. I was simply told to have faith in the message of the Bible. Do not question the Bible—do not doubt, just believe. However, I have come to realize that such blind acceptance is a dangerous way to approach life. There are indeed certain issues where you must "trust but verify" . . . particularly when the stakes are so high.

When it comes to issues of spiritual truth and spiritual reality, it becomes our responsibility to validate our sources and ensure they are indeed "reliable."

So we are left with the question, Is the Bible a reliable source? I cannot prove that it is the word of God, as one can prove that a mathematical equation is true. I can and will, however, in the chapters to come, give you some reasonably compelling evidence that should be helpful... particularly when you see all of the evidence, all of the research that undergirds the validity of the scriptures. It is in all likelihood some of the same evidence that led C. S. Lewis and Anne Rice to abandon atheism and ultimately believe the Bible is God's written revelation, a most reliable resource in which to place their trust.

A very unlikely candidate to validate these thoughts on the relationship between faith and reason is the famous French skeptic Jean Paul Sartre. He's probably one of the most prominent atheists to live in the last century. And over the course of his life he had put his faith in atheism. That's what he had believed to be true. But at the end of his life, he began to waver in that belief, and thirty days before he died, he shared these words in a published interview,

> The world seems ugly, bad, and without hope. There, that's the cry of despair of an old man who will die in despair. But that's exactly what I resist. I know that I shall die in hope . . . the only problem is . . . hope, faith needs a foundation.[8]

Sartre is saying that faith and belief must have a foundation to undergird it; otherwise it's blind faith. It's blind speculation.

In his classic book, *Green Letters*, Miles Stanford states that true faith must be based on that which is true and factual. As a Christian, he believes that a valid spiritual faith can be and is anchored in biblical facts and biblical truth. He writes, " . . . unless our faith is established on facts, it is no more than conjecture, superstition, speculation, or presumption." Bottom line? Stanford is telling us that faith without a strong foundation is nothing more than blind faith . . . and blind faith is worthless. However, he makes it clear that Christians do not have a blind faith—their trust is firmly anchored in the words of scripture. The Bible's validity is the very foundation of the Christian faith.[9]

Think about it in these terms. A skater can have a very low level of confidence in a sheet of thick ice that spans the winter lake before him, but in spite of his lack of faith in such thick ice, it will nonetheless hold him up just fine. In the alternative, however, that same skater can have enormous faith in the strength of the thin ice before him, yet when he sets out on this thin ice he will drown. You see, it's not the amount of faith you muster upfront (in fact, Jesus says, such faith may be as tiny as a little mustard seed)—it's your judgment in investing the faith you do have in something solid and true.

Faith has to have a strong foundation.

Millar Burrows served as the Department Chairman of Near Eastern language and literature at Yale Graduate School and became one of the world's great authorities on the Dead Sea Scrolls. Listen to this observation he made,

> There is a type of Christian faith . . . rather strongly represented today . . . which [is] not dependent on reason or evidence. [Many Christians] are often skeptical as to the possibility of knowing anything about the historical Jesus, and seem content to dispense with such knowledge.

Burrows goes on to say,

> I cannot share this point of view. I am profoundly convinced
> that the historic revelation of God and Jesus of Nazareth
> must be the cornerstone of any faith that is really Christian.
> Any historical questions about the real Jesus who lived in
> Palestine nineteen centuries ago is therefore fundamentally
> important.[10]

A good example of the importance of this is when kids, who have been
raised in the church, leave for college. They may believe the Christian
message but few will have a solid intellectual foundation to bolster their
beliefs. They will go off to college and their faith will be challenged by many
of their professors. Without anything to stand on, these young adults have
no response to the brilliant men and women who choose to tear their faith
apart in the classroom.

As a Christian, how imperative it is to know why we believe what we
believe? It all starts with the Bible. *So, is the Bible valid? Is it historically
reliable? Is it the word of God?*

THE UNIQUENESS OF THE BIBLE

Before we proceed to answer these questions, I would like to point
out several of the unique features of the Bible that will be helpful and
constructive, features not to be found in the sacred works of literature in
other cultures.

The great scholars of the world who have knowledge of ancient history
and ancient literature will generally agree that the Bible is unique in a number
of ways. When compared with the holy books of other world religions, we
find, for example, that the Bible stands apart from the *Koran*, which was
written in a very limited timespan and by one man. The *Bhagavad-Gita*,
which is Hindu, was also written by one man in a limited time span. *The
Book of Mormon*, also written by one man. And, finally, Buddhists don't
have a "sacred text," since they don't even believe in God; they keep adding
to it and then brushing it aside like sand at the doorstep. They add and take
away, they don't have a single source.

The Bible, however, is not just a single book. It is actually a collection of sixty-six books, all of which together is called the canon of scriptures. These sixty-six books contain a variety of genres—history, poetry, prophecy, wisdom literature, letters, apocalyptic, just to name a few.

Second, these sixty-six books, are written by forty different authors. These authors came from a variety of different backgrounds: shepherds, fisherman, doctors, kings, prophets, and others. And most of these authors never knew one another personally.

Third, these sixty-six books were written over a period of fifteen hundred years. Yet again, this is another reminder that many of these authors never knew or collaborated with one another while writing these books.

Fourth, the sixty-six books of the Bible were written in three different languages. In the Bible, we have books that were written in the ancient languages of Hebrew, Greek, and Aramaic—a reflection of the historical and cultural circumstances in which each of these books was written.

And finally, these sixty-six books were written on three different continents, Africa, Asia, and Europe. Once again, this is a testament to the varied historical and cultural circumstances of God's people.

Think about the above realities. Sixty-six books written by forty different authors over fifteen hundred years in three different languages on three different continents. What's more, this collection of books shares a common story line. The creation, the fall, and the redemption of God's people.[11]

Philip Yancey has some interesting words on this unique feature of the Bible.

> I find it remarkable that this diverse collection of manuscripts written over a period of a millennium by several dozen authors possesses as much unity as it does. To appreciate this feat, imagine a book begun five hundred years before Columbus and now just completed. The Bible's striking unity is one strong sign that God directed its composition. By using a variety of authors and cultural situations, God developed a complete record of what he wants us to know. Amazingly, the parts fit together in such a way that a single story does emerge.[12]

THE POWER OF THE BIBLE

In all the research I've done, and having read the Bible extensively, what really strikes me is how the biblical narrative seems to truly have spiritual power behind it. As St. Paul said about the message of the Bible, it "did not come to you in word only, but also in power."

You can see the transforming power of the Bible in the life of Émile Cailliet. He was born in a small town in France. He grew up agnostic, with no religious instruction of any kind. Until he turned twenty three, he had never even seen a Bible.

He served on the front lines in World War I and witnessed unspeakable atrocities. He reached a point where he truly believed he was destined to perish. As he reflected on the miserable condition he found himself in, he realized how inadequate his views were on the human condition. And he happened to be standing next to his best friend who took a bullet in the chest and died.

Cailliet was later wounded himself and confined for quite some time while recovering in the hospital. After he recovered, he returned to his graduate studies and began to think back on his experiences in the war.

> During long night watches in the foxholes I had in a strange way been longing—I must say it, however queer it may sound—for a book that would understand me. But I knew of no such book.[13]

He therefore decided to strike out on his own, and write his own book, a book that would explain the human condition. He collected writings and passages that seemed to fit into his book. As time passed, he looked forward with great anticipation for the opportunity to read this precious anthology that would help him understand himself.

The day arrived; he sat down under a tree and began to read, only to experience a sobering disappointment. He realized that instead of speaking to his true condition, these passages only reminded him of the context in which he had chosen them at various times in the past. His life now was so very different from those younger years. Cailliet realized that "the whole undertaking would not work, simply because it was of my own making."

That same day, as he returned home, dejected and dispirited, he found that his wife had come into possession of a Bible. While strolling their child in a baby carriage, she had encountered a minister who handed her a Bible that was written in French. Though Cailliet had been adamant that religion would be taboo in their home, he eagerly grabbed it from her. He recalls:

> I literally grabbed the book and rushed to my study with it. I opened it and "chanced" upon the Beatitudes. I read, and read, and read—now aloud with indescribable warmth surging within . . . . I could not find words to express my awe and wonder. And suddenly the realization dawned upon me. This was the book that would understand me! I needed it so much, yet, unaware, I had attempted to write my own—in vain. I continued to read deeply into the night, mostly from the Gospels. And, lo and behold, as I looked through them, the One of whom they spoke, the one who spoke and acted in them, became alive in me.[14]

Cailliet eventually became a Christian. He went to seminary and became a professor at the University of Pennsylvania and then Princeton Theological Seminary.

Dr. Mary Poplin had a similar experience. She teaches philosophy and learning theory, and for years she said she had pursued secular philosophies, particularly radical feminism and new age religion. She eventually found them empty and wanting, so she decided to investigate the New Testament. Not only would she read it but to really absorb it she chose to write it out by hand word-for-word. This is what she said about the experience,

> I felt my mind begin to heal. I felt clean and was healed. This word is a hitchhiker's guide to the whole cosmos. Especially life on one amazing blue planet. Its author refines our vision of himself and ourselves. Not only does he reveal himself as the maker of the heavens and the earth, but even more so as the lover of our souls. In all the literature I've read, it was the Bible that described with piercing precision, my human heart, my angst, and the pathos of the human condition. "Where can I run from your spirit," I asked along with David in the Psalms. Jesus taught his disciples to pray "forgive us our debts as we forgive our debtors." He knew my secret desire to condemn. He knew I could not forgive on my own strength. The Author knew I needed more than an abstract Veritas. I needed a human one living with and in me. "The Lord is close to the broken hearted and saves those who are crushed in spirit," Psalms 34:18 says. Though the Bible is calming and lovely, I knew it was not primarily a book of

poetry and literature, but a book claiming to be the real story in which we live asking the reader to taste and see that the Lord is good, offering to prove itself true. And so, it is full of verifiable information, useful to every person as well as to archeologists, historians, scientists, healers, artists, lovers, parents, and so on. If it is false, we can find out and go on to something else. But if it's true, we have sufficient basis for wise choices and for hope in this world.[15]

THE WISDOM OF THE BIBLE

Finally, the Bible also has an incredible wisdom to it that is timeless and applies to all people in all times. As Ravi Zacharias has noted,

> Biblical truth is trans-cultural. It has an indispensable message for modern man.[16]

The Bible has the ability to speak into people's lives and touch their souls. Not only does it reveal a great deal about the nature of God, but it also reveals a great deal about our human condition. It helps us understand ourselves, and, as the writer of Hebrews says, it reveals the thoughts and intentions of the heart.

Perhaps a clear example of God's wisdom speaking into the life of a man can be found in Dr. Francis Collins, one of the most prominent scientists alive today. Collins graduated from the University of Virginia with a degree in Chemistry. He received his PhD in Chemistry at Yale and then decided for good measure, he'd go to medical school at the University of North Carolina. From there, he returned to teach at Yale and later at the University of Michigan. He is most noted for being chosen to chair the Human Genome Project where, in 2003, he led an international collaboration of two thousand scientists in sequencing the human genome. More recently he was appointed by President Obama to be the Director of the National Institute of Health. Clearly, a very prominent scientist, but what is perhaps most interesting is his spiritual journey.

He began this journey as an atheist. In his third year of medical school, while he was working in the hospital, he was attending a woman who had really run out of options. She had a heart condition and, basically, was going to die soon. Collins was moved by this very kind and very faithful woman. She had a strong faith and she shared it with him.

She said, "You know, I'm ready to go. Don't worry about me."

And then she said, "Dr. Collins, you've been so kind to listen to me and care for me and listen to me share with you about my faith. Tell me about your faith. Tell me what you believe." Collins said,

> Nobody had ever asked me that question before, not like that, not in such a simple, sincere way. I realized I didn't know the answer. I felt uneasy. I could feel my face flushing. I wanted to get out of there. The ice was cracking under my feet. All of a sudden, by this simple question, everything was a muddle.[17]

Collins began to wonder if he was an atheist because he had chosen this position on the basis of reason or because it was the answer he wanted. He says it finally came to him,

> As a scientist, I had always insisted on collecting rigorous data before drawing a conclusion. And yet, in matters of faith, I had never collected any data at all. I didn't know what I had rejected. So I decided that I should be a little better grounded in my atheism. I better find out what this is all about. So I challenged a patient of mine who also was a Methodist minister. And after listening to my questions and realizing I was not dealing with a very full deck of information, he suggested that I read the Gospel of John, which I did . . . I found the scripture to be interesting, puzzling, and not at all what I had thought faith was about . . . then I began to read C.S. Lewis and realized there was a great depth of thinking and reasoning that could be applied to the question of God.[18]

Lewis convinced him that reason and faith go hand in hand, though faith has the added component of revelation—the Bible. Like C.S. Lewis, Collins had previously believed that Jesus and the stories of the Bible were nothing more than mere myths. Again, as he studied the historical evidence, he was stunned at how well documented and how historically accurate the Bible was. He also saw a surprising fidelity of the transmission of the manuscripts that were passed down over the centuries. And over time, Francis Collins, based on the accumulation of all the evidence he observed, concluded that God exists, that Jesus is the Son of God, and that the Bible is the means God has chosen to reveal himself to us. He also concluded that most of the religious skeptics that he knew, and that he meets today were just like he was. That is to say, they didn't want to think about these things and never looked at any evidence, never drawing conclusions from the real evidence that was available.

ONE THING CERTAIN

What so often happens in our lives when we encounter evidence that contradicts a long held belief is that we will pretend the conflict does not exist. We choose to become willfully blind, and in the process become irresponsible in what we believe.

This is what Dr. Dallas Willard, a distinguished philosophy professor at the University of Southern California, believes is a major problem with intellectuals who consider themselves to be agnostic or atheist. Willard finds that so many students and scholars he encounters on campus and out in the world are guilty of what he calls "irresponsible disbelief." These bright men and women often choose to disbelieve in something without any significant commitment to an investigation of that disbelief by way of sound reasoning and careful examination of the evidence.[19]

Do we not care about what is true? Are we afraid to look reality in the eye because it may take us in a direction we don't want to go? I believe this is one of the great flaws in our human character. We stubbornly hold on to our beliefs because they generally reflect how we *want* life to be rather than how life *actually is.*

So often, human beings let their preconceived theories and beliefs shape the way they see evidence. However, if we are people with intellectual integrity, we must allow the evidence to shape our theories and beliefs. We must ask ourselves this crucial question. Do we love the truth? Are we willing to follow it wherever it might lead us? Or are we guilty of irresponsible disbelief, where our beliefs are not based on the truth of evidence but on what we find to be appealing to our desires and biases?

Dr. Francis Collins, who acknowledges that he was clearly guilty of an irresponsible disbelief, became a seeker. But he will also tell you that he found the ultimate spiritual reality of life because he followed the dictum of Socrates: *follow the truth wherever it leads.* Collins found the truth and the foundation of that truth, for him, was in the Bible.

One thing is certain: if we do not have a great love of the truth, we most certainly will never find it.

TWO

THE HISTORICAL RECORD

*The only way we can know whether an event can occur is to
see whether in fact it has occurred. The problem of "miracles,"
then, must be solved in the realm of historical investigation, not in
the realm of philosophical speculation.*

– John Warwick Montgomery
Lawyer, professor, theologian, and author

THE HISTORY OF A FACT

Now, let's consider the nature of historical proof.

Forty-seven years ago, in February of 1966, I was in the sixth grade. I was twelve years old and played in a basketball game. I played for Highlands Elementary School and we played against McElwain Elementary.

McElwain was not very good and it was one of those days, where everything goes right for you. Now I was not a great basketball player, I was just average. As I tell my two boys, Dixon and Will, I could shoot, I just couldn't dribble. That's the challenge in basketball: you've got to be able to do both. But it was one of those days when every shot I launched went in, and I ended the day scoring twenty points. Probably the only time I ever scored in double figures.

Now imagine you are a detective. Someone comes to you and hires you to prove that this event actually happened—someone looking for proof that Richard Simmons scored twenty points forty-seven years ago.

As you set out to prove this, it is highly unlikely that you would go to a scientist or a philosopher to assist you in the effort. However, you might begin your research by going to people who knew me as a young boy and asking, Did Richard play basketball as a kid? And you would find them all tell you he loved basketball. He played all the time, and he was always out in the back yard shooting.

You might then go to McElwain Elementary. Quite frankly, I don't even know if it exists anymore. But it should not be too difficult to find out if there really was a school named McElwain that existed forty-seven years ago. Did they have a basketball team? A sixth grade basketball team? In 1966? You could go to my elementary school, Highlands, and you could find out if Richard Simmons III was indeed enrolled as a student forty-seven years ago. You would most likely be able to find, and thus prove, all of these facts to be true. Then you might go to some of my teammates, who, as far as I know, are all still alive. A number of them even in this town. You could go to them and ask them, all eyewitnesses, Do you remember that day? Let's assume several of these eyewitnesses say, Yes, I do remember that day; he was out of his mind, the way he was shooting.

And, since this was a YMCA program, let's say you find out that the Shades Valley YMCA still has in its basement all of the scorebooks from the youth basketball games of the past. As you go through them, you find the year 1966, you find February, sixth grade basketball, you find the Highlands vs. McElwain game and then you see the name Simmons. Nine baskets, two free throws, twenty points.

Let me ask you this question. Based on all of this evidence, could you conclude, reasonably, that I scored twenty points forty-seven years ago against McElwain Elementary?

You see, that is the nature of historical proof. This is what historical inquiry is all about. To prove something historically, historians must discover past events by piecing together evidence and interviewing eyewitnesses. As the noted historian, John Warwick Montgomery said, it is in the historical arena where we have to accept probability in historical judgments, based on the historical records and the evidence that is available.

AN ATTESTING MIRACLE

Probably one of the most respected books on man's diverse spiritual longings is *The World's Religions* by Huston Smith. Written in 1958, it is still regularly used in many college curriculums. Commentator Bill Moyers suggests it is one of the best books on comparative religion because of its objectivity and its sensitivity to all religious beliefs and practices. Smith, who was very well-educated, didn't have any particular religious leaning. He was unbiased. And in the book, in the section on Christianity, he begins with these words,

> Christianity is basically a historical religion. That is to say, it is founded not on abstract principles but in concrete events, actual historical happenings.[20]

Out of all the religions that Smith covers, he doesn't say this about any of the other world religions. The Bible, he suggests, unlike most of the world's great religious literature and traditions, is not centered on a series of moral, spiritual, and liturgical teachings, but, rather, on what God did in history and what he revealed in history.

The historical record does not seem to be of as much importance in other world religions. For instance, a number years ago, theologian Paul Tillich, hosted a conference in Asia with various Buddhist thinkers. During the conference he asked a simple question: What if by some fluke Siddhartha Gautama, the Buddha, had never lived and turned out to be some sort of fabrication? What would be the implications for Buddhism? The scholars all agreed that if Buddha had not existed, it would not matter. The reason, they concluded, is because Buddhism should be judged as an abstract philosophy, a system for living. They said it did not matter where the teaching originated.[21]

Christianity, on the other hand, requires an origination, a set of hard facts on which to stand. To make the point more explicitly, Peter Moore, the founder of Trinity Seminary, emphasizes that Christianity is the *only* world religion to make spiritual truth depend on historical events. And English historian and author Paul Johnson bolsters this truth by stating, "Christianity is essentially a historical religion. It bases its claims on the historical facts it asserts. If these are demolished it is nothing."[22]

When you read the Gospels, Jesus is often challenged by the religious leaders to give them a sign, telling him, We've heard all these great things about you. We've heard about these miracles you seem to have been performing. Well, we want to see one, too. We want to see something spectacular.

Jesus refuses to give them a sign. However, he promises throughout his ministry to give them a sign in the future . . . that he would die and rise again after three days.

And we should note that the translation of the word "sign" in the Greek literally means "an attesting miracle." They want an attesting miracle. They want Jesus to perform for them. Yet, Jesus refuses to perform on their terms and likewise we know that God will not perform on our terms today.

But what Jesus does say is remarkable in its impact for man. He says I am going to give you a sign, an attesting miracle. It won't be a scientific discovery, it won't be a philosophical argument, but, he says, it will be a single event that will take place during my lifetime. It will occur at the end of my life here on earth, and it will be a historical event. In fact, the Bible says, at the proper time he came into the world and he died. And he predicted he would rise again. That will be the attesting miracle. That is why the historical record is of such critical importance, and, why the attesting miracle that Jesus said he would provide would have to be proven historically.

IF I CAN'T PROVE IT, IT MUST BE WRONG

Christians believe that as wonderful as Jesus' life and teachings were, they are meaningless if they're not historically true.

In fact, the apostle Paul said that if the resurrection did not actually happen, if it did not take place, the Christian faith is worthless. Because of this, many a scholar over the years, have set out to prove that the resurrection never really happened, knowing that if they were to do so, it would demolish Christianity. But no one has been able to do it. In fact, there are any number of scholars who have written books on the subject, who surprisingly set out with that very objective—to prove Christianity a fraud—but in the process became Christians. Josh McDowell, Lee Strobel, Frank Morrison, to mention but a few.

For centuries, scholars have approached the Bible as they would any other ancient historical text. They ask the right questions that any historian would ask. Did this event really take place? Did it happen as described? What are the sources and are they reliable? What primary evidence is available? And these are all legitimate questions.

These are questions I began to think about almost thirty years ago when I stumbled upon a history book on ancient Rome. It was at a used book sale, and as I was browsing around I found an old textbook on Roman history. I bought it and took it home and found there was a section on Tiberius

known predecessor or successor, suddenly anticipated the whole technique of modern novelistic, realistic fiction.[24]

In other words, the writers of the New Testament would have had to come up with a deliberate series of lies, put them in writing, and then send them out to be read throughout the entire Roman Empire. These same men then would go out and die for these lies.

It is hard to believe that these early Christians would intentionally conspire to write lies, die for those lies, and then have such an influence that a large movement would form that would eventually transform the Roman Empire.[25]

Peter Kreeft, Boston College scholar and eminent philosopher, poses a very penetrating question when he asks, Why would the apostles lie? What would be their motive? People generally lie because somehow it will benefit them or keep them out of trouble. Kreeft suggests that in truth they could expect to get very little out of this,

> Misunderstanding, rejection, persecution, torture, and martyrdom? Hardly a list of perks.[26]

Now, one of the most common questions asked is why are there not more non-biblical historians who lived during this time who wrote about Jesus. There are two logical responses.

The first is that Jesus lived in Palestine, the most desolate part of the Roman Empire. It was an agrarian region where few people could read or write. They depended on the Jewish religious leaders for that, and of course, the Jewish religious leaders didn't look on Jesus very favorably. However, there are some ancient documents that refer to Jesus as a sorcerer who led the Jews astray. In fact, professor M. Wilcox, who wrote a very scholarly work called *Jesus in the Light of His Jewish Environment*, says this,

> The Jewish traditional literature, although it mentions Jesus only quite sparingly, supports the Gospel claim that he was a healer and a miracle worker even though it ascribes these activities to sorcery. In addition, it preserves the recollection that he was a teacher and that he had disciples and that at least in the earlier Rabbinic period, not all the sages had finally made up their minds that he was either a heretic or a deceiver.[27]

But this led Craig Blomberg to respond,[28]

> This acknowledges that he really did work marvelous wonders, although the writers dispute the source of his power.

A ROAD TO ROME

The second response is that there were, in fact, a large number of non-Biblical historians who lived during this time and who did write about Jesus. In his book, *The Verdict of History*, historian Gary Habermas, details a total of thirty-nine ancient sources. These are sources that document the life of Christ. Some of these were Christian historians, but many of them were not. To put this into perspective, there are only nine ancient sources that mention Tiberius Caesar. Only nine. Here we find an emperor of Rome who ruled for twenty-two years, yet there are only nine ancient sources that mention him while there are thirty-nine sources that speak of Jesus. Of these thirty-nine, several mention Jesus in just a paragraph or two while others write of him extensively. Let me share some words from three of them.

The first was Cornelius Tacitus. He was born in 57 A.D. and was ultimately considered the greatest historian of the Roman Empire. The *Cambridge Book of Ancient History* says Tacitus's writings are by far the most comprehensive and reliable ancient source of information of the Roman government, particularly during the time of Tiberius. Tacitus wrote a history of Rome and, during the time of Nero, he wrote about the emperor's villainous decision to burn Rome to the ground. Listen to these words of Tacitus,

> Consequently, to get rid of the report, Nero fastened the guilt and inflicted the most exquisite tortures on a class hated for their abominations, call Christians by the populace. Christus, from whom the name had its origin, suffered the extreme penalty during the reign of Tiberius at the hands of one of our procurators, Pontius Pilatus, and a most mischievous superstition, thus checked for the moment, again, broke out not only in Judaea, the first source of the evil, but even in Rome, where all things hideous and shameful from every part of the world find their center and become popular.[29]

Here, Tacitus corroborates the existence of Jesus: that his followers are called Christians, that he was executed by Pontius Pilate, and that he lived during the reign of Tiberius Caesar.

Justin Martyr, a second historian, lived from 65 A.D. to 110 A.D. We read this description of the early church. He writes,

> . . . on the day called Sunday there is a gathering together to one place of all those who live in cities or in the country and the memoirs of the apostles or the writings of the prophets are read as long as time permits.[30]

Martyr, who was a Christian historian, often quotes the four gospel writings from the New Testament, and he begins his citations with these important words, "It is written" or "God has said." You see therefore, at a very early date, the Gospels were recognized to have spiritual authority.

And, finally for our purposes, probably one of the most interesting writings about Jesus comes from a Jewish historian, Flavius Josephus, born in 37 A.D. He's touted as the greatest Jewish historian of antiquity. He's famous for a work that is now known as *The Antiquities of the Jews*. And in this massive work are these controversial words, which I will explain. It is important to note, at this point, that the words are clearly attributed by all scholars to Josephus. Josephus writes,

> About this time, there lived Jesus, a wise man, indeed if one ought to call him a man, for he was one who wrought surprising feats and was a teacher of such people to accept the truth gladly. He won over many Jews and many of the Greeks. He was the Christ. When Pilate, upon hearing him, accused by men of the highest standing amongst us, had condemned him to be crucified, those who had in the first place, did not give up their affection for him. On the third day, he appeared to them restored to life for the prophets of God had prophesied these and countless other marvelous things about him. And the tribe of Christians, so called after him, has still to this day, not disappeared.[31]

Josephus was born right at the time that Christ died. Clearly, Josephus makes these remarks about Jesus as the above words are included in all the ancient copies in *The Antiquities of the Jews*. But the controversy arises because Jewish scholars and now many Christian scholars believe that there are a couple of interpolations contained in the text. An interpolation occurs when a copyist inserts some phrase or phrases that a Jewish writer like

Josephus would not have written. Josephus, of course, was Jewish, he wasn't a Christian, and yet the text states that Jesus was "the Messiah." Josephus, as a practicing Jew, would most certainly not have said that Jesus was "the Messiah." However, in other places Josephus says that Jesus was "called the Messiah," which is something a Jewish historian would most likely say. In other words, Josephus as well as any person of the time could have said that people "called" Jesus the Messiah with or without actually having "belief" in Jesus as the Messiah.

Now when Josephus writes of the resurrection on the third day, *he appeared to them, restored to life*, this writing most likely, according to most scholars, actually meant, *his disciples and the early believers allege that he rose again on the third day*, and that's the way history presents it now.

Yet, nevertheless, Edwin Yamauchi, one of our country's leading experts in ancient history, says that Josephus clearly wrote the words in question. There's no doubt about the authorship, Yamauchi writes, and even if there are interpolations,

> Josephus corroborates important information about Jesus, that he was the martyred leader of the Church in Jerusalem, and that he was a wise teacher who had established a wide and lasting following, despite the fact that he had been crucified under Pontius Pilate, at the instigation of some of the Jewish leaders.[32]

If we had no New Testament, and all we had was ancient secular history, this is what we would know about Jesus,

- Jesus lived during the time of Tiberius Caesar
- He lived a virtuous life
- He was a wonder worker
- He had a brother named James
- He was acclaimed to be the Messiah
- He was crucified under Pontius Pilate
- He was crucified on the eve of the Jewish Passover
- Darkness and earthquake occurred when he died
- His disciples believed he rose from the dead
- His disciples were willing to die for their belief
- Christianity spread rapidly as far as Rome
- His disciples denied the Roman gods and worshipped Jesus as God.

Edwin Yamauchi comments,

> Put all this together—Josephus, the Roman historians and
> officials, the Jewish writings, the letters of Paul and the
> apostolic fathers—and you've got persuasive evidence that
> corroborates all the essentials found in the biographies of
> Jesus. Even if you were to throw away every last copy of
> the Gospel, you would still have a picture of Jesus that's
> extremely compelling; in fact, it's a portrait of the unique
> Son of God. [34]

Dr. Norman Geisler, a brilliant philosopher, who received his PhD from
Loyola University and who was an author of over sixty books, says this runs
even deeper because of what it says about the New Testament. He says here
you have these ancient secular historians, collectively revealing a storyline,
congruent with the New Testament record. He says,

> Beginning in February of A.D. 303, the Roman emperor
> Diocletian ordered three edicts of persecution upon Christians
> because he believed that the existence of Christianity was
> breaking the covenant between Rome and her gods. The
> edicts called for the destruction of churches, the destruction
> of all manuscripts and books, and the killing of Christians . . .
> Hundreds, if not thousands of manuscripts were destroyed
> across the Roman empire during this persecution which
> lasted until A.D. 311 . . . Even if Diocletian had succeeded
> in wiping away every Biblical manuscript off the face of the
> earth, he could not have destroyed our ability to reconstruct
> the New Testament. Why? Because the early Church Fathers,
> such as Justin Martyr, Irenaeus, Clement of Alexandria,
> Origen, Tertullian, and others, quoted the New Testament
> so much, in fact, 36,289 times to be exact, that all but eleven
> verses of the New Testament can be reconstructed just from
> their quotations.

> In other words, you could go down to your local public
> library, check out the history books of the early Church
> fathers, and read nearly the entire New Testament, just from
> their quotations of it. So, we have not only thousands of
> manuscripts, but also thousands of quotations from those
> manuscripts.[35]

IT'S ALL IN THE DETAILS

In the New Testament, Luke is the author of the book of Luke as well as the book of Acts. These books together comprise a total of fifty-two chapters, approximately 20 percent of the New Testament. In both books you find incredible detail. Luke was a physician and historian who based his reporting on testimony received from eyewitnesses. In the book of Acts, particularly the last twelve chapters, he is himself an eyewitness. And as you read the book of Acts, you see an impressive array of knowledge of local places, people's names, as well as social conditions, customs, and circumstances—clearly information described by an eyewitness who had been there.

Classical scholar and historian Colin Hemmer chronicles Luke's accuracy in the book of Acts verse by verse with incredible detail. In the last sixteen chapters of Acts, he identifies eighty-four facts that have been confirmed by historical and archeological research. (These eighty-four historical facts can be found at the back of the book in Appendix Five.)[36]

Sir William Mitchell Ramsay is considered to be one of the greatest archeologists in history. He performed most of his work across Asia Minor and the Middle East. An Englishman, he was raised an atheist; the son of atheists of great wealth. Receiving his doctorate in archeology from Oxford, he committed his entire life to archeology and set out for the Holy Land with the intention of undermining the validity of the Bible. His hope was to completely discredit the book of Acts. He was confident he could do so because there was simply so much historical information he believed he could draw upon.

> I began with a mind unfavorable to it [Acts] . . . It did not lie then in my line of life to investigate the subject minutely; but more recently I found myself often brought into contact with the book of Acts as an authority for the topography, antiquities, and society of Asia Minor.[37]

Over time, Ramsay was forced to completely reverse his beliefs as a result of the overwhelming evidence uncovered in his research. After thirty years of vigorous and comprehensive study and analysis, this is what he had to say about Luke's ability as a historian,

> Luke is a historian of the first rank; not merely are his statements as facts trustworthy . . . this author should be

placed along with the very greatest of historians . . . .Luke's history is unsurpassed in respect to its trustworthiness.[38]

These are strong words and are of vital importance. Remember the foundational principle we started with at the beginning of this chapter? Christianity is the only world religion where spiritual truth depends on the veracity of clearly defined and discoverable historical events.

Eventually, after uncovering many hundreds of artifacts confirming the historicity of the New Testament record, Ramsay, would shock the archaeological community when he revealed to the world that he had become a Christian.[39]

THREE

THE ARCHEOLOGICAL RECORD

It is not now the men of faith; it is the skeptics . . . who have reason to fear the course of discovery. (Citing the mounting number of archeological findings in support of the biblical accounts.)

– Paul Johnson
Historian

THE FREEDOM TO LOVE

A loving God would certainly desire to reveal himself to his creation—his thoughts and his wisdom to his people—but why has he limited his communication to the written word as the primary means of this communication? With all the attendant troubles with writing and language issues—translations and semantics and varied interpretations of meaning—why wouldn't he just speak and let his presence be known here in the modern world? Why can't we have that kind of demonstration from God?

It is important to point out though that the written word has not been God's exclusive method of expression. For example, we read throughout the biblical record that God for some reason chose to speak audibly to certain individuals like Abraham, Moses, Job, and the apostle Paul. The clearest expression we have of course is the revelation of Christ himself, God in the flesh, coming into the world. As the scripture says, the truth became flesh and dwelt among us and we were able to behold the physical presence of his glory. In and through this person Jesus, God spoke audibly into people's lives.

There are a number of reasons God speaks into the minds and hearts of people through the scriptures, through the written word. The primary reason is that if the infinite God of the universe regularly spoke audibly to us, we would be terrorized into loving and listening to him. Such a direct and demonstrative communication would create a situation in which God virtually forces himself on mankind. Serving and listening to him would become compulsory. There is no freedom in compulsion; and love cannot be generated out of terror.

The great Danish philosopher Søren Kierkegaard examined this issue and gave great insight into it by sharing a wonderful parable. It is the parable of a young king, who was single and desired a queen. His palace overlooks the marketplace, and one day he sees a young peasant girl come out to do her shopping. He's quite taken by her beauty and her easy smile. He notices how kind she is to everyone and how they light up when she says hello. She walks to a food stall, buys some food, and, then, she disappears. The king is quite taken by her, yet, she has no idea that the king of this country has any idea who she is.

The next day, he looks for her and again he sees her. Before long, he looks for her every day at the same time out in the marketplace. One day he realizes that he is hopelessly in love with this peasant girl, who has no idea he has been watching her. Now he realizes that as king, as the sovereign of this country, he could force her to marry him and be his wife and queen. Yet, he also realizes that forcing her won't really make her love him, and, he would never know if she truly loved him. And so he makes the decision to take off his crown, take off his royal clothes, and dress as a peasant. The king goes out to win her love, knowing she just might reject him.

The young king proves his wisdom in recognizing that true love exists only when we choose to love from a condition of freedom. And this is what the God of the Bible chose to do. He sent his son, from his throne of glory, into the world as a mere man. In the process, Jesus served as God's special revelation, also demonstrating his great love for mankind.

Philip Yancey, in his book *Disappointment with God*, offers some powerful insight on this, recognizing that God's open demonstration of power in the Old Testament did not encourage spiritual development. In fact, the Israelites in the desert had no need of faith at all. God's clear presence took away freedom, making every choice that confronted them a matter of obedience and not faith.

God did not play hide-and-seek with the Israelites; they had every proof of his existence you could ask for. But astonishingly—and I could hardly believe this result, even as I read it—God's directness seemed to produce the very opposite of the desired effect. The Israelites responded not with worship and love, but with fear and open rebellion. God's visible presence did nothing to improve lasting faith.[40]

Shortly after I came upon Yancey's insight, I happened to come across a biblical expression of this same human tendency in the book of John. Jesus, after performing many miracles, including raising Lazarus from the dead, a miracle witnessed by large numbers of people, was not received as one would have expected,

> But though he had performed many miracles before them, yet they were not believing in him. (John 12:37)

God, in his omniscience, does not regularly appear in a visible, powerful way, but, I might add, he has not hidden himself. He can be found by any who truly seek him, and, in fact, he makes this promise to mankind,

> If you seek me, you will find me.

Through the recorded truth of the Bible, God continues to reveal himself to us. He relates to us, in one sense, in the same way the wise king of that parable expresses his love to the peasant girl. By coming into the world as one of us. In doing so, God reveals himself to us by demonstrating his love in a most extraordinary way—by forfeiting his life on the cross, rising from the dead, and leaving us with the written word as testament of that truth.

Christianity, as we have discussed earlier, is, by its own defining principles, a rigorous historical faith. For this reason, Christian scholars must demand accuracy in the historical record. And, as we have determined, the Christian faith firmly rests upon proven historical events, especially, the life, death, and resurrection of Christ.

And since history is a record of the past, based on testimony, history demands that events and happening be recorded and documented. In essence, this is the only way for history to be preserved. All we have is five thousand years of recorded human history and if it is going to be preserved it's got to be written down. There's got to be a record.

Yet there is another kind of "writing" available to us that validates the

Bible's historicity—it appears in the field of archeology, where structures and cultural artifacts are "read" by experts in one of the most modern fields of interdisciplinary scholarship. Archeology combines science, history, engineering, language, and sociology.

DIGGING HISTORY, FINDING FAITH

I read an interesting excerpt about archeology from Oliver Wendell Holmes,

> I believe in the spade. It has fed the tribes of mankind. It has furnished them water, coal, iron, and gold. And now it is giving them truth—historic truth, the mines of which have never been open till our time.[41]

A spade, used in former times just as a hand tool, is likewise used today as a digging device for farming and gardening, but to the modern archeologist it has a special use. In many ways it is like a pen or a typewriter or a computer . . . removing dirt from ancient earth and constructing a story from the landscape and the objects that are revealed.

What's important to realize is that archeology is considered a relatively young science. It is understood as a branch of historical research that seeks to reveal the past by a systematic recovery of surviving remains. What I find to be quite fascinating is that for many years archeology had no great value to historical scholarship. Most archeologists, for so many of the early years, were like the fortune hunters in the movie *Raiders of the Lost Ark,* looking for treasures—gold, art objects, relics that would bring great wealth. They were looking for ways to get rich quick.

But all that has changed. Now, we have this large field of study called archeology, including the discipline of biblical archeology, focusing, of course, on education, decipherment, and critical evaluation of ancient materials and records related to the Bible and biblical times.

What's important to know is that one hundred years ago, many scholars believed that the Bible told the history of a mythological world. Sort of like C. S. Lewis providing a detailed fictional account of the history of Narnia, or like J. R. R. Tolkien writing a fictional genealogy of the Hobbits and all who dwelled in Middle Earth. Many early twentieth century scholars believed the Bible was unrelated to real people and events; it was all made up, a great story written to explain what was beyond their knowledge base.

And the reason so many skeptics blieved this was because there was no real archeological remnants to support the actual history of the accounts. Where do we see any physical "writing" that mentions or, for that matter, suggests that Moses and King David, two of the great personalities in the biblical account, even existed? Where are any mentions or remnant objects from this or that battle determining the fate of Israel and God's people?

But again, all that has changed, particularly in the last century, and it's critical to understand the important role archeology plays in validating the scriptures. Archeology will not and cannot prove the Bible to be the Word of God. However, when archeologists dig throughout the Middle Eastern part of the world and find ancient sites that are consistent with where the Bible said we would find them, then they are able to "read" these ancient sites and determine whether its history and its geography are biblically accurate.

Listen to the words of Dr. John McRay, who has written a rich and deeply comprehensive book on archeology in the New Testament,

> . . . this is what archeology accomplishes. The premise is that if an ancient historian's incidental details check out to be accurate time after time, this increases our confidence in other material that the historian wrote but that cannot be as readily cross-checked.

And as far as recent archeological discoveries go, McRay concludes,

> There is no question that the credibility of the New Testament is enhanced.[42]

The credibility of any ancient document is enhanced when you excavate and find the author was accurate when describing a particular place or event. For example, up until 1993, there had been no archeological discovery that confirmed the existence of King David, who was one of the most crucial figures in the Old Testament. In fact, more is probably written about David in the scriptures than anyone other than Jesus. Then, on July 21, 1993, all of that changed.

KING DAVID

The award-winning journalist, Jeffery Sheler, in his book *Is the Bible*

True? informs us,

> It was July 21st, 1993, and the workday was nearly over for the team of Israeli archeologists excavating the ruins of the ancient Israelite city of Dan in upper Galilee. The team, led by Avraham Biran of Hebrew Union College in Jerusalem, had been toiling since early morning, sifting debris in a stone-paved plaza outside what had been the city's main gate.
>
> Now, the fierce afternoon sun was turning the stoneworks into a reflective oven. Gila Cook, the team's surveyor, was about to take a water break when something caught her eye—an unusual shadow in a portion of recently exposed wall along the east side of the plaza. Moving closer, she discovered a flattened basalt stone protruding from the ground with what appeared to be Aramaic letters etched into its smooth surface. She called Biran over for a look.
>
> As the veteran archaeologist knelt to examine the stone, his eyes widened. "Oh, my God!" he exclaimed. "We have an inscription!"
>
> In an instant, Biran knew that they had stumbled upon a rare treasure . . . In his twenty-seven years at the site, Biran had found other inscriptions, but none like this one. Most consisted of a few letters of Aramaic, Hebrew, or Greek etched onto tiny potsherds, the popular "notepads" of the ancient Near East. One important fragment unearthed in 1976 identified the site as the biblical city of Dan, the strategic northern outpost mentioned prominently in the books of 1 and 2 Samuel, 1 and 2 Kings, and 1 and 2 Chronicles.
>
> But this discovery, as Biran suspected when he first saw it, would prove to be far more significant. It would make the front page of the *New York Times* and touch off a heated debate in the often arcane world of biblical scholarship. The basalt stone was quickly identified as part of a shattered monument, or stele, from the ninth century BCE, apparently commemorating a military victory of the king of Damascus over two ancient enemies: the king of Israel and the house of David. As it would be translated later, the twelve partial lines of inscription read || . . . *my father went up* . . . || *and my father died, he went to [his fate . . . Is-] . . .* || *rael formerly*

in my father's land . . . || I [fought against Israel?] and Hadad
went in front of me . . . || . . . my king. And I slew of [them X
footmen, and Y cha-] || riots and two thousand horsemen . . . ||
the king of Israel. And [I] slew [. . . the kin-] || g of the House
of David. And I put . . . || their land . . . || other . . . [. . . ru-]
|| led over Is[rael . . .] || siege upon . . .[43]

Sheler continues, writing that the fragmentary reference to David was an immediate historical bombshell,

> Never before had the familiar name of Judah's ancient warrior king, a central figure in the Hebrew Bible and, according to Christian Scripture, an ancestor of Jesus, been found in the records of antiquity outside the pages of the Bible. Skeptical scholars had long seized upon that fact to argue rather persuasively within the biblical academy that David was a mere legend, invented, they said, like much of Israel's biblical history, by Hebrew scribes during or shortly after Israel's Babylonian exile (roughly five hundred years before the start of the common era). David and presumably other heroes of the Hebrew Bible, the skeptics argued, were about as historical as King Arthur.
>
> "There are no literary criteria for believing David to be more historical than Joshua, Joshua more historical than Abraham, and Abraham more historical than Adam," British biblical scholar Phillip R. Davies had argued just a year before the discovery at Dan. "There is no non-literary way of making this judgment either since, none of these characters has left a trace outside of the biblical text!"
>
> But with Biran's startling discovery, the skeptics' argument has suffered a serious blow. Now, at last, there was material evidence, an inscription written not by Hebrew scribes, but by an enemy of the Israelites a little more than a century after David's presumptive lifetime. It seemed to be a clear corroboration of the existence of King David's dynasty and, by implication, of David himself.[43]

What most people don't realize is that since 1948, archeologists have discovered over one hundred thousand relics in Israel and the most significant relics are those with inscriptions like the one that I just described.

THE POOL OF SILOAM

This next discovery was first reported in the United States in August of 2005, so you can see how relatively new this science is. This was reported in the *Los Angeles Times*,

> Workers repairing a sewage pipe in the old city of Jerusalem have discovered the biblical Pool of Siloam, a freshwater reservoir that was a major gathering place for ancient Jews making religious pilgrimages to the city and the reputed site where Jesus cured a man blind from birth, according to the Gospel of John.
>
> "The pool was fed by the now famous Hezekiah's Tunnel and is 'a much grander affair' than archeologists previously believed, with three tiers of stone stairs allowing easy access to the water," said Hershel Shanks, editor of the Biblical Archeology Review, which reported the find Monday.
>
> "Scholars have said that there wasn't a Pool of Siloam and that John was using a religious conceit 'to illustrate a point,'" said New Testament scholar James Charlesworth of the Princeton Theological Seminary.
>
> "Now we have found the actual Pool of Siloam . . . exactly where John said it was. A gospel that was thought to be 'pure theology' is now shown to be grounded in history," he said.
>
> When the ancient workmen were plastering the steps before facing them with stones, they either accidentally or deliberately buried four coins in the plaster. All four are coins of Alexander Jannaeus, a Jewish king who ruled Jerusalem from 103 to 76 B.C. That provides the earliest date at which the pool could have been constructed.
>
> Similarly, in the soil in one corner of the pool, they found about a dozen coins dating from the period of the First Jewish revolt against Rome, which lasted from A.D. 66 to 70. That indicates the pool had begun to be filled in by that time.
>
> "Because the pool sits at one of the lowest spots in Jerusalem, rains flowing down the valley deposited mud into it each winter. It was no longer being cleaned out, so the pool

quickly filled with dirt and disappeared," Shanks said.[44]

THE HITTITES

This third example is of vital importance because it relates to the book of Genesis and the other early books of the Old Testament. Many scholars believe that Genesis is truly all fiction. It's mythology; it's all made up.

In the Old Testament, there existed a people called the Hittites, who are mentioned forty-seven times. They were one of many nations listed who inhabited the land of ancient Canaan when Abraham first entered the lands. (Genesis 15:20). They also were mentioned to have purchased chariots and horses from King Solomon (1 Kings 10:29). They maintained such a powerful army that the king of Israel hired them to fight the powerful Arameans (2 Kings 7:6,7). And in 2 Samuel 11 we read about the most famous of the Hittites, Uriah, a soldier in King David's army. Uriah was married to Bathsheba, with whom David had an adulterous affair.

However, despite the number of times the Hittites are mentioned, for so many years, critical scholars doubted they ever truly existed. There was no historical evidence that proved their existence . . . at least not until certain clay tablets were discovered among the ruins of an ancient city in Turkey called "Boghaz-Koy." This prompted German archeologist Hugo Winkler to go to the site and further excavate the area where these tables had been found. There he found a room with over ten thousand clay tablets. Here is how archeologist Randall Price describes it,

> Once they were finally deciphered, it was announced to the world that the Hittites had been found. Boğazköy had, in fact, been the ancient capital of the Hittite empire known as Hattusas. Other surprises followed such as the revelation that the Hittites language should be classed with the Endo-European language, of which English is a part, and that form of their law codes was very helpful in understanding those described in the Bible. The rediscovery of this lost people, one of the most outstanding achievements in near-Eastern archeology, now serves as a caution to those who doubt the historicity of particular Biblical accounts. Just because archeology has not produced corroborating evidence today does not mean it could not tomorrow. The Hittites are just one example in which the Bible has been shown to be historically reliable. Thus, it should be respected despite

the present lack of material support for certain events and chronological problems that remain unsolved.[45]

THE WORD "POLITARCH"

One final example comes from the book of Acts, chapter 17, verse 6. Luke the historian and author of the book of Acts, uses a term to describe the city officials in Thessalonica. It's the Greek word "politarch." And this is the only place in ancient literature where that word is ever found.

Many skeptical scholars contend this is proof that Luke did not know what he was writing about and could not be trusted as a historian. But once again, archeologists have found the word "politarch," and it wasn't found scattered throughout the Roman world. It was found in one place—the city of Thessalonica. Sixteen inscriptions of this very word were found, and one was even discovered on an arch that was once above one of the gates of the city.

Clearly, this was a term unique to the city of Thessalonica and it demonstrates Luke's extraordinary power of observation and his reliability as a historian. [46]

In his book *Rational Conclusions*, James Agresti provides a list of some of the most important cities, towns, landmarks, and people that are referred to in the Bible and which are corroborated by the archeological record. In Appendix IV, at the back of the book, you will find a sampling of these discoveries. Although this is not an all-inclusive list, it will give you an idea of the significant amount of archeological support for the historicity of the Bible.

On the contrary, the archeological record has proven to be a great challenge to other religions. A good example is Mormonism. Joseph Smith, the founder of the Mormon Church, claimed that *The Book of Mormon* is the most flawless of any book upon the earth. However, archeology has repeatedly failed to substantiate any of its claims about events that purportedly occurred long ago in the Americas. The Smithsonian Institute says,

> There is no direct connection between the archeology of the new world and the subject matter of *The Book of Mormon*.[47]

As authors John Ankerberg and John Welden concluded in a book on the topic of Mormonism,

No *Book of Mormon* cities have ever been located. No *Book of Mormon* person, place, nation, or name has ever been found. No *Book of Mormon* artifact, no *Book of Mormon* scriptures, no *Book of Mormon* inscriptions, nothing . . . has ever been found.[48]

FIND AFTER FIND

Biblical archeology as a science, as history, as a discipline continues to add to man's understanding of the past. What is so interesting is that each time that archeology sheds new light on the Bible, the biblical record gains greater validity and trustworthiness as a historical document, and, in turn, proves it to be a useful tool for the archeological community at large.

For instance, Yigael Yadin, who directed the excavation at Hazor in the 1950s, relied heavily on the Bible's guidance in finding the great gate of Solomon at the famous upper Galilee site. He said,

> We went about discovering [the gate] with Bible in one hand and spade in the other.[49]

Trude Dothan, whose work centers on the Philistines notes that,

> . . . without the Bible, we wouldn't even have known that there were Philistines.[50]

And then there is William Dever who argued earlier in his career that archeology and the Bible each should keep a safe distance from each other. He since has completely changed his mind and now firmly believes,

> All archeologists working in Israel must have sound training in Biblical studies in order to properly understand the context of their work.[51]

The archeological discoveries in the last seventy-five years have certainly excited the public and perhaps even stunned many skeptics. This method of searching for truth has brought archeology to a place where it supports the biblical record and the biblical text.

I'd like to turn to author and journalist Jeffery Sheler, who wrote a compelling article in the *U.S. News and World Report*, called *The Mysteries of the Bible*, and who has spent so much time and research on biblical archeology,

> Now the sands of the Middle East are yielding secrets hidden for thousands of years that shed surprising new light on the historical veracity of those sacred writings . . . Some have even hailed the discoveries as the beginning of a new "golden age" of Biblical archaeology.[52]

Kenneth Kitchen, the noted historian and archeologist, who taught at the University of Liverpool and is one of the leading experts on biblical history and the Egyptian third intermediate period, says this,

> There is quietly mounting evidence that the basic inherited outline of biblical history is essentially sound.[53]

One of the great biblical archeology professors in the world is Dr. John McRay. Having received his doctorate in archeology from the University of Chicago, he taught archeology at the graduate level for over thirty years at Wheaton College and also served as a consultant for *National Geographic Magazine*. In an interview he was asked if he had *"ever encountered an archeological finding that blatantly contradicts a New Testament reference?"*

McRay shook his head and said, *"Archeology has not produced anything that is unequivocally a contradiction to the Bible."* He continued with confidence,

> On the contrary, as we've seen, there have been many opinions of skeptical scholars that have been codified into fact over the years but that archeology has shown to be wrong.[54]

Dr. William Albright the legendary professor and archeologist at Johns Hopkins, had this to say,

> The Bible no longer appears as an absolutely isolated monument of the past, as a phenomenon without relation to its environment.[55]

* * * * *

The excessive skepticism shown towards the Bible by important historical schools of the eighteenth and nineteenth centuries has been progressively discredited. Discovery after discovery has established the accuracy of innumerable details and has brought increased recognition of the value of the Bible as a source of history.[56]

Albright was not a Christian. He was an unbiased archeologist, and he tells us that the Bible has value as a "source" of history, and the presumption of truth can be applied to much of its historical basis.

And, finally, probably one of the greatest archeologists of the twentieth century was a college president and rabbi named Nelson Glueck. His extraordinary accomplishments include the discovery of approximately fifteen hundred archeological sites in the lands of the Bible. He was featured on the cover of *Time Magazine* for his archeological endeavors and when John F. Kennedy was sworn in as president of the United States, Glueck delivered the benediction. Based upon decades of archeological research, Dr. Glueck penned this momentous statement,

> It may be stated categorically that no archeological discovery has ever controverted a Biblical reference . . .[and further arguing] . . . the almost incredibly accurate historical memory of the Bible, and particularly so when it is fortified by archaeological fact.

And this is why James Agresti, after all of his research in his book *Rational Conclusions*, says,

> I have yet to encounter archeological evidence that shows any part of the Bible to be inaccurate.[59]

Truly a powerful statement and it appears that modern biblical archeology concurs with this assessment.

THE ANCIENT WRITINGS

There is no body of ancient literature in the world
which enjoys such a wealth of good textual attestation
as the New Testament.

– F. F. Bruce
Distinguished Scholar on the life of Paul,
former President of the Society for Old
Testament Study as well as the Society for
New Testament Study

THE ROLE OF THE RELIABLE SOURCE

It struck me that what I am trying to accomplish in this book is to take the various pieces of a puzzle and put them together in a simple and clear manner in order to answer the question, Is there a good reason to believe that the Bible is the Word of God? I am convinced that true faith has to have a foundation; the stronger that foundation, the greater the faith. So many skeptics and religious naysayers think Christians have nothing but blind faith; and, in reality, blind faith is worthless.

Here is a good illustration that might be beneficial in understanding the difference between a "strong faith" and a "blind faith." A good friend is standing in front of you with his right hand in his pocket. Your friend tells you he has something in his pocket and that this object is in his right hand. If you were asked to guess what was in his hand, you would most likely think of the options for a minute or two and then take a few wild guesses.

But after another minute or so, you'd resign yourself to the fact that any further attempts would be fruitless—the object in your friend's hand could be a multitude of things and you are simply wasting time as you continue to wildly guess.

Just guessing is rarely effective when facing steep odds. That's what blind faith is—coming to a certain conclusion based on no evidence, with absolutely no empirical data.

Now if your friend tells you that he has a fifty dollar bill in his hand, you now have evidence. Assuming that your friend is trustworthy, you can believe that he has a fifty dollar bill in his hand, even though you cannot see it. This is what faith is. To repeat Augustine's words, "Faith is trust in a reliable source." The more reliable and trustworthy the source, the stronger a person's faith will be.

As Christians, we must put our faith in what we are told by the writers of scripture, by the prophets, by the apostles, by Jesus himself . . . and so 'that's where we're putting our trust. It is not a blind faith, and this is why we must ask the question, How trustworthy is the Bible? How trustworthy are those who wrote the Bible? How do we know what we have today has been passed down to us faithfully over the centuries?

Finally, once your friend takes his hand out of his pocket and reveals to you that, yes, there is a fifty-dollar bill in his hand (he wasn't joking or lying), you now have a true knowledge of what was in his pocket. Similarly, the Bible tells us that one day we will see God as he really is, and we won't have to operate by faith. We will have a true, complete knowledge of him.

There are a number of reasons why God has chosen to speak into our lives through the written word. Written statements, written communication can be transmitted from one reliable source to the next, from one generation to the next, with the highest likelihood of accurate and precise communication—both across languages, geography, and time. In other words, a speaker's intention is most clearly understood when it's written down, or, in today's world, filmed or recorded.

Here is a humorous illustration of the need for reliable sources by Ravi Zacharias,

> A student was finishing up his PhD by writing his dissertation. He did not, however, like how dissertations were judged.
>
> In his paper, instead of using credible sources, he would make a profound statement and say, "as told to me by a waiter at a Fifth Avenue restaurant." And then he would

make a statement, "as told to me by a taxi driver." All verbal references to someone he had talked to.

His professor confronted him on this practice and said, "You can't make statements like this in a dissertation. You have to have written references or footnotes. It's got to be verified."

The student asked, "Why? Why do you have to have written references? Why does it have to be written if I got it from a waiter or taxi driver who spoke it to me?" He was trying to make a mockery of the dissertation process.

The professor, said, "Well, that's all right. If that's the way you feel. I'm just trying to figure out where you're coming from."

On the day of graduation, the professor informed him that he had passed him. "We're going to award you your PhD," he said, "but we're not going to give it to you in writing. You get no written diploma . . . You just take my word for it."[60]

You see, documentation is crucial when it comes to history and truth propositions. Through our earlier discussion of history and archeology as pieces in our puzzle, the Bible, as a collection of multiple documents, offers yet another truth proposition, and this is why the biblical documents have been handed down to us with such great care over the passage of time. Even so, there are many people who are not aware of how carefully the Bible has been passed down to us without error or modification. Without such knowledge, it is easy to see how modern people so easily believe that the biblical documents, being so ancient, have been dramatically changed or altered over the centuries.

ANCIENT DOCUMENTS

Ancient Christian documents (including, of course, the Bible) when compared to the number and quality of all other ancient written documents shed a unique and surprising light on the nature of historical truth.

Ravi Zacharias, a teacher and philosopher, a brilliant biblical commentator, says,

> The biblical documents have withstood the most scrutinizing analysis ever imposed upon any manuscript and have emerged with compelling authenticity and authority. No other ancient literature demonstrates such a high degree of accuracy.

What gives Zacharias the confidence to make such a forthright statement?[61]

Generally speaking, in the field of ancient history, you will find no original manuscript, only copies that have survived. Not a single one of the many writers we know from the past—Aristophanes, Homer, Plato, Socrates, Ovid, Livy, Archimedes, Euclid, for example—have an extant original from their time. You will not find an original manuscript that was actually written by any of these authors. What we have are copies of the originals.

Copying manuscripts from one generation to the next is the only way ancient written documents like the Bible could have survived—but I would point out that this is not an issue that is unique to the Bible. All documents that have come down to us from antiquity have been transmitted through handwritten copies. Up until the second century A.D., virtually all literature, all written works, were primarily copied on material called papyrus, which was made from a plant or reed, and they would glue them together like you would plywood. And this paper-like product was then rolled around wooden cylinders to form what are called scrolls.

The problem with papyrus, as you can probably imagine, is that they had a relatively short life-span. They would easily disintegrate over time because they were vulnerable to moisture. Eventually, papyrus was replaced by parchment, which was made from animal skins and was much more durable.

Parchment, however was much more difficult and costly to produce and, therefore, was rather scarce. As a result, it ended up being used almost exclusively for documents which were considered to be of greatest importance. And by the fourth century A.D. almost everything was written on parchment as it became the primary material that scholars used in their work. For this reason, some of the oldest books we have in our possession today were written on parchment.[62]

DO YOU COPY?

Over the centuries, ancient documents were copied and recopied as they were passed down from one generation to the next. In the mid-1400s, Gutenberg invented the printing press, which radically changed the world. What most people do not know is that up until this time, when the printing press was invented, there were only around thirty-thousand books that existed in all of Europe. And what's interesting is that nearly all of these thirty-thousand works were Bibles or Bible commentaries meticulously recorded by monks over the centuries. How did this happen?[63]

When you look back on the history of Rome, between the second and fifth centuries, the Roman Empire was in decline. Because of this decline Rome was highly vulnerable to attack by outsiders. In 395 A.D., the Roman Empire was split in to two separate entities. The Western Roman Empire and the Eastern Empire, which was called the Byzantine Empire. One hundred years later in the fifth century, the Barbarians invaded and left the Western Roman Empire in shambles.

In fact, it is hard to believe that this very civilized part of the Empire had completely disintegrated. Their cities were reduced to ruins and there was little left of Roman power, society, and culture. It just disappeared. And it triggered a five-hundred-year period that historians call the Dark Ages.

It's hard to picture this part of the world, which had once been ruled by law and order—with such great intellectual pursuit and trade—merely disintegrating into a state of anarchy. It was during these Dark Ages, in this part of the world, when one could find no academic pursuits except for the work done by Christian monks in monasteries. And it was these monks who preserved the scriptures and much of the classical literature we have available today. Over time, Christian schools, libraries, and monasteries began to grow and flourish, particularly under the patronage of King Charlemagne from 768 to 814. It was during his reign that the Church was strengthened. Charlemagne placed intense effort on copying and preserving all of the ancient documents in their possession, and, since Christianity places such great emphasis on wisdom and knowledge, the Church's preservation efforts to secure and copy new documents became its highest priority.

It's interesting to note that ancient classical literature owes its survival today to Christianity and the Church. When we turn to the Byzantine Empire, we find a highly advanced multi-cultural society which for the most part remained Christian and existed for more than a thousand years.

Christian scholars from this era and from this diverse culture not only preserved the Bible during these centuries, but also copied many of the secular Greek and Latin classics and much of the Jewish literature we have today.[64]

A question, I often encounter is how do we know that what we read in the Bible today conforms to the original documents when all we have are copies of the originals?

Well, scholars who study ancient history will tell you that in order to test the validity of any ancient literary work you have to consider two criteria. The first is to look at how many manuscripts exist (and when I say manuscripts, I'm talking about written documents, hand-written documents) that were copied prior to the printing press. So, you have to consider the number of ancient manuscripts we have in our hands today, manuscripts that you can look at and examine. The greater the number of manuscripts would indicate a greater accuracy of the writings in question.

Take Plato for instance. My closest friend from college was a political science professor for years and taught political philosophy. In one of his introductory courses he required his students to read Plato's *Republic*. And he will tell you there is no scholar alive who questions the validity of that work. And yet, when you consider Plato, all we have is 7 manuscripts.

And take Aristotle, for example. We only have 49 of his manuscripts.

And Homer's *Iliad*. We have 643 copies of his manuscripts.[65]

But when you consider the New Testament, just the New Testament alone, we have 5,300 manuscripts written in the original Greek. We have over 10,000 Latin manuscripts of the entire New Testament, and we have 9,300 portions of the New Testament. In other words, we have over 24,000 manuscripts.[66]

Let's also consider that in addition to these 24,000 manuscripts there are additional writings. James Agresti, author of *Rational Conclusions*, says,

> Early Christian writers from the second century onward quoted from the books of the New Testament so profusely that even if there weren't a single New Testament manuscript in existence, the vast majority of it could be reconstructed from the writings of these early Christians.[67]

Do you grasp what he's saying? He is affirming that all of the additional written material substantiates the exact language of the manuscripts copied during this early Church history, particularly from the first, second, and third centuries. The early Christian fathers wrote profusely and quoted consistently from the books of the New Testament. Just from their writings alone you could reconstruct the whole New Testament!

NUMBERS TELL THE STORY

Now, you may ask, why is the *number* of manuscripts so significant? Dr. Bruce Metzger, a Greek New Testament scholar who taught at Princeton Theological Seminary, a real authority on the ancient Greek manuscripts of the New Testament, says that when you have a large number of manuscripts from different geographical areas and different languages, you can cross check them to determine what the original documents were like. And he says, when you compare a manuscript that was copied in 300 A.D. with one that was copied in 900 A.D. you can determine if they are the same documents by a simple examination of the wording.[68]

John Wenham, another Greek New Testament scholar and author of the highly regarded book, *The Elements of New Testament Greek*, says when you compare the great diversity of copies of New Testament manuscripts, you will find them all to be "relatively homogenous." They appear to be almost the same, and this is why Metzger believes that the resulting text we have today is 99.5% accurate to the originals, and that that .5% in question does not affect a single doctrine.

James Agresti, an engineer who designed Jet engines, was a staunch atheist for many years. He does not say why, but he took a year to carefully read the Bible, studying the objective evidence for its accuracy. This is what he concluded,

> In summary, the evidence for the textual accuracy of the New Testament books is overwhelming. With the exception of about two paragraphs in the entire New Testament, the manuscript evidence is so strong, there is no rational basis for any kind of uncertainty over the substance of the text.[69]

It was this evidence that played a major role in him becoming a Christian.

And then Dr. Norman Geisler says this,

> In fact, the New Testament documents have more manuscripts, earlier manuscripts, and more abundantly

supported manuscripts than the best ten pieces of classical literature combined.[70]

It seems to be quite clear that an overwhelmingly large number of New Testament manuscripts sufficiently demonstrates how fundamentally stable and accurate the reproduction of the biblical text was from the early first century to the invention of the printing press, a span of more than fourteen hundred years.

TIME PROVES THE POINT

It is apparent therefore that the number of ancient manuscripts we have in our possession today is important. Yet there is a second critical criterion that helps us to validate classical literature: Determining the time span between the writing of the original manuscript by the original author and comparing it to the oldest copy that we have in our possession today. Scholars who study ancient writings operate on the principle that the shorter that time gap, the more accurate the manuscript. For instance, if I wrote something in 100 A.D., and the oldest copy that we have available today was copied in 500 A.D., that would be a four-hundred-year time gap.

Now let's go back to the four examples we have considered thus far.

Plato. Plato lived between the years 427 and 347 B.C. He probably did most of his writing in the last twenty years of his life. The oldest copied manuscript we have in our hands today was copied in 900 A.D. So we have a 1,200-year gap between the original work of Plato and the oldest copies we have in our possession today.

Aristotle lived between 384 and 322 B.C. The oldest copied manuscripts we have in our possession today were copied in 1100 A.D. A 1,400-hundred-year gap between the original work and the oldest copies we have available today.

Homer, who was clearly the most widely read author in antiquity, wrote *The Iliad* in around 900 B.C. The oldest copy we have in our possession today was copied in 400 B.C. We only have a 500-year time gap there.[71]

So we have Plato, a 1,200-year gap; Aristotle, 1,400 years; and Homer, 500 years.

Now, the twenty-seven books of the New Testament were written between 40 A.D. and 100 A.D.

They weren't all written at the same time, and it is natural to ask how we know this. How do we know the actual dates of when the New Testament books were written?

There are a number of ways actually. The early Church father, Clement of Rome, for instance, a well-regarded historian, wrote a letter to the Corinthian church dated 95 A.D. In this letter he quotes verses from the four Gospels—from the book of Acts, the book of Romans, I Corinthians, Ephesians, Titus, Hebrews, and 1 Peter. There are several of these types of letters indicating that the entire New Testament was written in the first century A.D.[72]

Amy Orr-Ewing in her book *Why Trust the Bible?* shares some interesting insights on the dating of the New Testament books,

> There is, of course, other internal evidence for a first-century date for the writing of the New Testament. The book of Acts ends abruptly with Paul in prison awaiting trial. (Acts 28: 30, 31) It is likely that Luke wrote Acts during this time, before Paul finally appeared before Caesar. This would be about A.D. 62-3, meaning that Acts and Luke's gospel were written within thirty years of the ministry and death of Jesus. Further evidence of this is that there is no mention of the destruction of Jerusalem in A.D. 70. Although Matthew, Mark, and Luke record Jesus' prophecy that the temple and the city would be destroyed within this generation [Matthew 24:1,2, Mark 13:1,2, Luke 21: 5-9, 20-24, 32], no New Testament book refers to this event as having happened. It is likely that letters written after A.D. 70 would have mentioned this fulfillment of Jesus' prophecy.[73]

In 70 A.D., there was a historic war between the Romans and the Jews. It lasted for a number of years and culminated with the Roman army attacking Jerusalem. It was a historic war because over a million people died in the siege of Jerusalem. And Rome prevailed, completely destroying the city. They also completely demolished the temple. Josephus called it the greatest war of all time. In fact, historians will tell you it was an unprecedented national, human, economic, and religious tragedy. And Jesus predicted it. But the destruction of Jerusalem is never mentioned in the New Testament. In fact, the New Testament speaks of Jerusalem, the temple, and the activities associated with them still intact at the time of the writing.[74]

Consider this example. If you were to read a book about the great buildings of the world and, in this book there is a discussion of the New York World World Trade towers, which ends with these words, "These two buildings are clearly the most economically productive structures in the world today." Once you read that line, you would know that it was written prior to September 11, 2001. And that is precisely why so many scholars believe the entire New Testament was written before 70 A.D., because in the books of the New Testament, Jerusalem and the temple are still intact.

Some liberal scholars think the New Testament wasn't written until hundreds of years after Jesus. However the oldest copy of the New Testament in our possession today is called the Rylands papyrus, which comprises a major part of the book of John copied in 130 A.D.[75] And, furthermore, we have an entire copy of the New Testament which was copied in 325 A.D.[76]

So using 70 A.D. as the completion date of the New Testament and the Rylands papyrus having been copied in 130 A.D., we have a sixty-year gap. A sixty-year gap!

This sixty-year time gap between the original writings and the oldest manuscript copies we have in our possession today has led many of the most prominent scholars to make comments such as this one by the noted historian and lawyer, John Warwick Montgomery,

> . . . to be skeptical of the resultant text of the New Testament books is to allow all of classical antiquity to slip into obscurity, for no documents of the ancient period are as well attested bibliographically as the New Testament.[77]

Princeton scholar Benjamin Warfield said,

> If we compare the present state of the New Testament text with that of any other ancient writing, we must declare it to be marvelously correct. Such has been the care with which the New Testament has been copied—a care which has doubtless grown out of true reverence for its holy words.[78]

And probably the most important quoted source to consider is Sir Frederic Kenyon. He was the director of the British Museum in London for many years, an honored and prestigious position to say the least. And in the last few decades before he died, we see that numerous papyri portions of the New Testament documents had been discovered, documents which were written at the end of the first century. And evaluating these discoveries just before he died, Kenyon concluded,

The interval, then, between the dates of original composition and the earliest extant evidence becomes so small as to be, in fact, negligible, and the last foundation for any doubt that the Scriptures have come down to us substantially as written has now been removed. Both the authenticity and the general integrity of the books of the New Testament may be regarded as finally established.[79]

Even the skeptical scholar John A. T. Robinson admits,

The wealth of manuscripts, and above all the narrow interval of time between the writing and earliest extant copies, make it by far the best attested text of any ancient writing in the world.[80]

THE DEAD SEA SCROLLS

The discovery of the Dead Sea Scrolls played a major role in validating the Old Testament records.

In 1947, a Bedouin shepherd boy named Mohammed was in search of a lost goat. As he was throwing rocks, one of them fell into a hole, and he was surprised to hear the shattering of pottery. He was on the west side of the Dead Sea about eight miles south of Jericho. He was hoping he had discovered a buried treasure, but he was disappointed to find it was nothing but a cave full of jars containing leather scrolls. They had been carefully sealed and, as it was later determined, had been there for almost two thousand years. Archeologists believe they were placed there in 68 A.D.[81]

As you can imagine, archeologists, journalists, and scholars flooded to the excavation site. For nine years they excavated the entire area. In the process, they found numerous scrolls, thousands of manuscripts, and a number of different fragments, all well-preserved in airtight clay jars. They'd been placed there, ironically, by a Jewish monastic society called the Essenes. And most scholars believe that they were hidden in these caves during the Jewish revolt against Rome—sometime between 66 A.D. and 73 A.D—as a protection against the Roman attack.

When these manuscripts were first discovered, those to whom the Bedouin shepherd boy had told his story were also disappointed. They, too, would have preferred treasure over manuscripts—but soon they realized that people would pay money for such discoveries. Fortunately, they sold them to credible individuals who valued them and who would ensure they were placed in the hands of universities, museums, and collections where they could be properly studied.

One important scroll in particular was the ancient Isaiah scroll, which was apparently copied around 100 B.C. This was such a significant discovery because prior to it, the oldest copy available of the Old Testament had been copied in the ninth century A.D. Thus, until this discovery, there existed a thousand-year time gap for the Old Testament, and this discovery shortened the gap so dramatically that it excited the interest of religion scholars all over the world. The people who possessed this copy of the book of Isaiah, trying to determine what they actually had in their possession, contacted the American School of Oriental Research in Jerusalem.[82]

An employee named John Trever, who had just received his PhD from the school, also happened to be an excellent amateur photographer. Trever took photographs of all the passages of the great Isaiah scroll, which measured twenty-four feet long and ten-inches high, and sent these images to Dr. William Albright, the leading biblical archeologist in the field. Having received the photographs, Albright studied them and concluded that the Dead Sea find is,

> [T]he greatest manuscript discovery of modern times! . . . And there can happily not be the slightest doubt in the world about the genuineness of the manuscript.[83]

And he dated the scrolls to approximately 100 B.C.

Award-winning freelance journalist Jeffrey Sheler covered the American religion scene for nearly two decades at *U.S. News and World Report.* He writes extensively about the Dead Sea Scrolls in his well-researched book, *Is the Bible True?* He writes,

> [When scholars] carefully examined the fragile parchment scrolls and assembled hundreds of brittle fragments into page after page of Biblical text, the scholars were astonished at what they found.[84]

Notre Dame professor Eugene Ulrich, who was an editor of a series called "Discoveries in the Judean Desert," comments,

> The scrolls have shown that our traditional Bible has been

amazingly and accurately preserved for over two thousand years.[85]

What biblical scholars ultimately discovered, then, was that the scrolls found in these caves were Old Testament manuscripts and fragments and they were virtual matches to copies written thousands of years later. But what may be of the greatest significance, unlike the many fragments discovered, is that they also possessed the Isaiah scroll, comprising the *entire* book—all sixty-six chapters—of Isaiah. It is over 2,100 years old today.

What is so amazing is how the text has undergone so little alteration as it was copied over the centuries. Norman Geisler suggests, for instance, to take the fifty-third chapter of the book of Isaiah, which many consider to be the most important chapter. It was written about a "suffering servant" who would bear the iniquity of the world.

> Of the 166 words in Isaiah 53, there are only seventeen letters in question. Ten of these letters are simply a matter of spelling, which does not affect the meaning. Four more letters suggest stylistic changes, such as conjunctions, and the remaining three letters are minor stylistic changes, such as conjunctions. The remaining three letters comprise the word "light," which is added in verse eleven (Isaiah 23: 11) and does not affect the meaning greatly.
>
> Thus, in one chapter, of 166 words, there is only one word (three letters) in question, after a thousand years of transmission, and this word does not significantly change the meaning of the passage.[86]

This demonstrates the great care that was given by those who copied it. In the Dead Sea Scrolls, there are portions of every Old Testament book except for the book of Esther.

So, can you see the significance of the Dead Sea Scrolls as they relate to the Old Testament? In addition, as James Agresti points out ...

> One of the primary facts revealed by the Dead Sea Scrolls is that the traditional text of the Old Testament has been transmitted very accurately for at least two millennia.[87]

Clearly, those who copied and recopied the Old Testament documents did so with great care and reverence. They believed they were performing a sacred task that would influence many generations to come. Here, Dr. Bernard Ramm describes their work,

> Jews preserved it as no other manuscript has ever been preserved. With their masora (parva, magna, and finalis) they kept tabs on every letter, syllable, word, and paragraph. They had special classes of men within their culture whose sole duty was to preserve and transmit these documents with practically perfect fidelity—scribes, lawyers, masoretes. Whoever counted the letters and syllables and words of Plato or Aristotle? Cicero or Seneca?[88]

For those who are interested in reading more about the ancient scriptural documents, you may find interest in a brief overview of the canonization process to see how the books of the Old and New Testaments were chosen to be included in the Bible. This can be found in Appendix III at the end of the book.

Lee Strobel, who has written a number of books, graduated from Yale Law School and became the legal affairs editor of *The Chicago Tribune*. He described himself and his wife, as, at that time, "decadent atheists," and, then, one night, everything changed,

> Leslie stunned me in the autumn of 1979 by announcing that she had become a Christian. I rolled my eyes and braced for the worst, feeling like the victim of a bait-and-switch scam. I had married one Leslie—the fun Leslie, the carefree Leslie, the risk-taking Leslie—and now I feared she was going to turn into some sort of sexually repressed prude who would trade our upwardly mobile lifestyle for all-night prayer vigils and volunteer work in grimy soup kitchens.
>
> Instead I was pleasantly surprised—even fascinated—by the fundamental changes in her character, her integrity, and her personal confidence. Eventually I wanted to get to the bottom of what was prompting these subtle but significant shifts in my wife's attitudes, so, I launched an all-out investigation into the facts surrounding the case for Christianity.
>
> Setting aside my self-interest and prejudices as best as I could, I read books, interviewed experts, asked questions, analyzed history, explored archeology, studied ancient literature, and for the first time in my life, I picked apart the Bible, verse

by verse.

I plunged into the case with more vigor than any story I had every pursued. I applied the training I had received at Yale Law School as well as my experience as legal affairs editor of the *Chicago Tribune* and over time the evidence of the world—of history, of science, of philosophy, of psychology— began to point toward the unthinkable.[89]

For his research, Strobel traveled all over the country interviewing scholars, which he records in several of his books. Once he began studying ancient manuscripts, he sought an individual whom he considered the top authority in this field, Bruce Metzger. Eighty-four years old at the time, Metzger was incredibly well-educated. He held a Master's and PhD from Princeton and another Master's from Princeton Theological Seminary, where he had also taught. He'd been awarded five honorary doctorates from five different colleges and had written scores of books. This is what Strobel says about him,

If you scan the footnotes of any authoritative book on the text of the New Testament, the odds are that you're going to see Metzger cited time after time. His books are mandatory reading in universities and seminaries around the world. He is held in the highest regard by scholars from across a wide range of theological beliefs.[90]

Strobel spent several hours with Metzger, and when the interview ended, they had this final exchange,

As we stood, I thanked Dr. Metzger for his time and expertise. He smiled warmly and offered to walk me downstairs. I didn't want to consume any more of his Saturday afternoon, but my curiosity wouldn't let me leave Princeton without satisfying myself about one remaining issue.

"All these decades of scholarship, of study, of writing textbooks, of delving into the minutia of the New Testament text—what has all this done to your personal faith," I asked.

"Oh," he said, sounding happy to discuss the topic, "it has increased the basis of my personal faith to see the firmness with which these materials have come down to us, with the multiplicity of copies, some of which are very, very ancient."

So, I started to say, *scholarship has not diluted your faith?*

He jumped in before I could finish my sentence. "On the contrary," he stressed, "it has built it. I've asked questions all my life, I've dug into the text, I've studied this thoroughly and today I know with confidence that my trust in Jesus has been well placed."

He paused while his eyes surveyed my face. And then he added for emphasis,

"Very well-placed."[91]

⇌ FIVE ⇌

THE REACH OF SCIENCE

My road to atheism was paved by science . . .
but, ironically, so was my later journey to God.

– Lee Strobel
Award-winning Journalist & Author

THE AGE OF REASON

I am not a man of science. In fact, I never really liked it much in school, but I have read a great deal on the subject matter contained in this chapter. What I am presenting is similar to a well-documented research paper, but it is, by the nature of my limitations as a scholar, at a level that people like you and I can understand.

What I have found to be true in the lives of most people—even some of the most well educated people—is that it is difficult to stay up-to-date on the world of science and scientific discovery. Many of us have neither the time nor the interest in pursuing and keeping track of the often obscure details of the vast world of scientific controversies. Unless your career intersects with the sciences in some very real and practical way, my guess is that much of what is contained in the chapter will be eye opening. It certainly was for me. Although it is true that our reason and our dreams can far exceed our reach, the question I propose to answer is, Are there limits to what we can and cannot know?

Most scholars will agree that the period in history we now call the Enlightenment has had the greatest influence on the world as we know it in the twenty-first century. Now, in the public sphere of life all activity and debate has to do with the world of facts. Most every public factor and decision must be governed by man's ability to reason and to think logically. But this move toward reason and *reason alone* has brought us to the slippery slope where many individuals are unquestioning in their belief that humanity can now, in fact, *master* nature. Consequently, we live in a world that has concluded there is no longer a need for divine revelation. God, we are instructed, has become irrelevant because human beings on their own can search out and know all the facts about reality. Therefore, religion has been relegated to private life, to be kept behind closed doors, because it is based solely on individual values and opinions—it is not factual.

The Enlightenment slowly shifted Western culture's perspective to the general understanding that reason could and, perhaps, should rule all aspects of how we consider and view our place in the world—confident that by human reason we would be able to discover all that is necessary to advance humanity towards its highest goals and aspirations. This is why science, for so many people, has now come to displace God.[92]

Many modern intellectuals argue that only science is rational and only science can lead us to the truth. They contend everything else in life is mere belief and opinion. And, of course, because belief and opinion can often be wrong, if something cannot be quantified and tested by the scientific method, it cannot be proven to be true.

However, many modern scholars are now concluding that there are a number of flaws with this limited worldview and that there remains much to learn and know that science may never be able to prove. As we have already discussed, the scientific method cannot prove that an event which took place in the past is in fact historically true. Science also cannot tell us what is moral and immoral, what is good and what is evil.

Listen to the words of Richard Dawkins, who is a scientist and probably the most prominent atheist alive today,

> There was a well-known television chef who did a stunt recently by cooking human placenta and serving it up as a pate, fried with shallots, garlic, lime juice and everything. Everybody said it was delicious. The father had seventeen helpings. A scientist can point out, as I have done, that this is actually an act of cannibalism. Worse, since cloning is such a live issue at the moment, because the placenta is a true genetic clone of the baby, the father was actually eating his own baby's clone. Science can't tell you if it's right or wrong to eat your own baby's clone, but it can tell you that's what

you're doing. Then you can decide for yourself whether you think it's right or wrong. [93]

Did you hear what he said? Science can't tell you if something is "right" or "wrong."

Or, perhaps we could frame the argument by thinking about this statement, "Feed the hungry." This certainly seems to be a morally compelling statement, whether you are Christian, atheist, Muslim, or Jew. Certainly, it is good to care for the poor and disadvantaged, but is it rational? Is there a scientific reason to do it? It seems to work against the law of natural selection. What does the scientist with hungry mouths to feed say is "moral" and "immoral" when push comes to shove and he finds himself confronted by starving people?

The prominent scientist, Francis Collins says,

> Science really is only legitimately able to comment on things that are part of nature. And science is really good at that, but if you're going to try to take the tools of science and disprove God, you're in the wrong territory. Science has to remain silent on the question of anything that falls outside of the natural world. [94]

Interestingly, Collins and Richard Dawkins had a debate in *Time Magazine*. In commenting on the debate, Collins, said,

> Basically, we went back and forth about a number of the issues, but I challenged him about how it was possible from a scientific perspective to categorically rule out the presence of God. At the end of the interview, he did admit that he couldn't, on a purely rational basis, exclude the possibility of a supernatural being. But, he says, such a being would be grander and more complicated and awesome than anything humans could contemplate. [95]

Collins said he wanted to shout out, You finally got it! Yes, that is the God of the Bible.

In his classic book *My View of the World*, Nobel Prize-winning physicist Erwin Schrodinger, the legendary co-architect of quantum theory, validates this argument,

> [Science] is ghastly silent about all and sundry that is really

near to our heart, that really matters to us. It cannot tell us a word about red and blue, bitter and sweet, physical pain and physical delight, knows nothing of beautiful and ugly, good or bad, God and eternity. Science sometimes pretends to answer questions in these domains, but the answers are very often so silly that we are not inclined to take them seriously. [96]

Probably one of the most influential scientists in the last fifty years, paleontologist Stephen J. Gould of Harvard, was a staunch defender of Darwinism and an outspoken atheist.

But [Gould] was very clear that it wasn't his science that brought him to that position. He argues in his very interesting book Rocks of Ages that science simply cannot, by the legitimate application of its method, comment on the God question. In other words, it simply lies beyond the scientific method. [97]

AN EVOLVING PICTURE

There seems to be three ways people view the relationship between science and God. The first is this: science and religious belief are at war with each other. That's the approach Richard Dawkins takes. And most people who share this view also believe that science has the overwhelming edge in credibility because it's about provable facts and religion depends on faith.

The second view is that science and religious belief have nothing to do with each other. In other words, they are two separate and distinct realms that don't intersect or interact at all. Steven J. Gould, believed that,

Science and faith occupy distinct, different domains. Science covers the empirical universe while religion extends to issues of morality and values.[98]

And a third way to view the relationship is that the testimony of science points, *it doesn't prove*, it *points* to the existence of God. There is a large number of credentialed and highly-respected professors, in all scientific disciplines—e.g., astrophysics, biology, medicine, sociology, archeology, chemistry, cosmology—who believe there is a very strong case for theism at the heart of the universe.

Dr. Steven Meyer, who has degrees in physics, geology, and a doctorate in history and philosophy of science, all from the prestigious Cambridge

University, says that,

> In fact, across a wide range of sciences, evidence has come
> to light in the last 50 years which, taken together, provide a
> robust case for theism. [99]

Dr. Allan Rex Sandage is considered the greatest observational
cosmologist in the world and has impeccable credentials. Sandage, a one-
time colleague and protégé of Edwin Hubble, the legendary astronomer who
first discovered the background noise proving that the big bang did indeed
occur, has received an impressive array of honors from such organizations as
the American Astronomical Society, the Swiss Physical Society, the Royal
Astronomical Society, and the Swedish Academy of Sciences (astronomy's
equivalent to the Nobel Prize).

Back in the 1980s, there was a very important conference held in Dallas,
and its purpose was to discuss the origin of the universe. The format would
seat a panel of scientists on one side of the room who believed in God and
the other side of the room you would have those who didn't. It was assumed
that Sandage would align himself with the atheists during the debate.
Knowing that he had been a virtual atheist since he was a child, there was
no doubt where he'd be sitting.

And then the unexpected happened: Sandage set the room abuzz
by turning and taking the chair among the theists. And what's even
more interesting is what he had to say about the big-bang theory and its
philosophical implications. Furthermore, he decided to disclose publicly at
this conference that he had become a Christian at the age of sixty.

The big bang, he told the rapt audience, was a supernatural event
that cannot be explained within the realm of physics as we know it. He
continued,

> It was my science that drove me to conclusion. . . . It was only
> through the supernatural that I can understand the mystery
> of existence . . . [100]

James Clark Maxwell was one of the most exceptional scientists who
ever lived. He left a legacy of accomplishments considered equal to those
of Einstein. He made significant contributions to diverse realms of physics,
but more important, he discovered the fundamental laws that govern
electricity, light, and magnetism. Max Plank, the founder of the discipline
of quantum physics, said that Maxwell achieved greatness unequalled.

Maxwell was leery of linking scientific theories to the Bible because he believed the truth in the Bible was absolute and unchanging whereas the theories in science were consistently changing, consistently in flux,

> I have looked into most philosophical systems and I've found that none will work without a God. The belief in design is a necessary consequence of the laws of thought acting on the phenomena of perception . . . For this reason Maxwell says, I put my "hope in Christ". [101]

Then there's Dr. John Baumgardner with a PhD in Geophysics and Space Physics from UCLA. In 1997, US News and World Report described him as the world's preeminent expert in the design of computer models for geophysical convection, the process by which the earth creates volcanoes, earthquakes, and the movement of continental plates.

> Science has flowed from a Christian understanding of reality, a Christian understanding of God, and a Christian understanding of the natural world. In general, I believe that science is legitimate, that it does reveal the glory of God, that it does confirm what the scripture says is valid and true. [102]

Probably the most celebrated intellectual who came to theism as a result of study (he has been described as the most notorious atheist in modern time), was the British philosopher Anthony Flew, who launched his attack against the idea of the existence of God in 1950 with a presentation at Oxford, "Theology and Falsification." Although for the next fifty or more years his philosophical writing would span a number of subjects, he nonetheless remains best known for his defining work on atheism in such books as *God and Philosophy*, *The Presumption of Atheism*, and *Atheistic Humanism*. Several years ago, however, he changed his position—he became a theist (not a Christian) and stunned the world, writing a remarkable book called, *There is a God: How the World's Most Notorious Atheist Changed His Mind*. In the book, he states,

> I now believe that the universe was brought into existence by an infinite intelligence. I believe that this universe's intricate laws manifest what scientists have called the 'Mind of God'. I believe that life and reproduction originate in a divine source. Why do I believe this; given that I expounded and defended atheism for more than a half a century? The short

answer is this—this is the world picture as I see it that has emerged from modern science. [103]

And then finally, probably the most well-known scientist alive today is physicist Steven Hawking. He has suffered from Lou Gehrig's disease for a number of years and is confined to a wheel chair. Crippled to near complete paralysis, he remains able to move a cursor with his right hand, which enables him to speak through the computer by transmitting digital key strokes to a voice synthesizer. Hawking has written a number of popular books but is remembered most for *A Brief History of Time*, perhaps the best-selling book on science ever written. Hawking says,

> The odds against a universe like ours emerging out of something like the Big Bang are enormous. I think there are clearly religious implications . . . . It would be very difficult to explain why the universe would have begun in just this way except as the act of a God who intended to create beings like us. [104]

Does the latest science seem to point to the existence of God? Could it be that science is itself evolving in the face of new discoveries, new evidence, and bold critical thinking? Can we detect a revived openness in the scientific community to the possibility of an ultimate creator? What are the facts? According to a survey of the members of the American Associate for the Advancement of Science conducted by the Pew Research Center in May and June of 2009, 51% of scientists said they believed in God or a higher power, while 41% said they did not. [105]

Much of the work of leading theoretical scientists in cutting-edge fields such as cosmology, particle physics, and nanotechnology (involving concepts such as quantum fluctuations, dark matter, the Higgs-Boson field, or tropistic behavior) actually coincides with three areas of traditional religious inquiry: the origin of the universe, the origin of life, and the origin of human life.

BIG BANG, BIG NEWS

Let's start with the origin of the universe. In the book of Genesis (Gen. 1:1), we're told that God created the heavens and the earth. And then in Romans 4:17 it says, "God calls into being that which does not exist." God, as an omnipotent creator, has the ability to bring into being that which does not exist, and, therefore, the universe has a beginning. However, for much of the last century, cosmologists believed the universe was eternal and one need not think about the origin of the universe because it didn't have a beginning. It has always existed.

But when Einstein came along with his theory of relativity, and then astronomer Edwin Hubble began his work observing the heavens, this view began to change.

> . . . it was 1916 and Albert Einstein didn't like where his calculations were leading him. If his theory of general relativity was true, it meant that the universe was not eternal but had a beginning. Einstein's calculations indeed were revealing a definite beginning to all time, all matter, and all space. This flew in the face of his belief that the universe was static and eternal. Einstein later called his discovery irritating. He wanted the universe to be self-existent, not reliant on any outside cause, but the universe appeared to be one giant effect. In fact, Einstein so disliked the implications of General Relativity, a theory that is now proven accurate to five decimal places, that he introduced a cosmological constant (which some have called a "fudge factor") into his equations in order to show that the universe is static to avoid an absolute beginning.

> By 1922, Russian mathematician Alexander Freidman had officially exposed Einstein's fudge factor as an algebraic error. (Incredibly, in his quest to avoid a beginning, the great Einstein had divided by zero something that even schoolchildren know is a no-no.) Meanwhile, Dutch astronomer Willem de Sitter found that General Relativity required the universe to be expanding. And in 1927, the expanding of the universe was actually observed by astronomer Edwin Hubble.

> Looking through the one hundred-inch telescope at California's Mount Wilson Observatory, Hubble discovered a red shift in the light from every observable galaxy, which

meant that those galaxies were moving away from us. In other words, General Relativity was again confirmed. The universe appears to be expanding from a single point in the distant past. [106]

In 1929, Einstein himself made a pilgrimage to Mount Wilson to look through Hubble's telescope. What he saw was irrefutable. The observational evidence showed that the universe was indeed expanding as general relativity had predicted. With his cosmological constant now completely crushed by the weight of the evidence against it, Einstein could no longer support his wish for an eternal universe. He subsequently described the cosmological constant as "the greatest blunder of my life." And he redirected his efforts to find the solution to the puzzle of life. Einstein said, and I quote, that he,

> . . . wanted to know how God created the world. I'm not interested in this or that phenomenon, in the spectrum of this or that element, I want to know his thought. [107]

Einstein went on to say, most likely with tongue in cheek, that the rest are just details.

The predominant view in cosmology today is the big-bang theory, which states that the universe is expanding from a single point in the distant past. In other words, at some definite point in the dimension of time there was a uniquely massive explosion, what scientists call a "singularity," and the universe has been expanding ever since. Thus, since the universe had an actual beginning, then, arguably, the big-bang theory points rather conspicuously to a theistic view of the universe.

The big bang is profoundly theistic.

In fact, I read recently that it is hard to find a cosmologist that will want to participate in a public debate on the existence of God. What's happened in their branch of science makes the atheistic point of view extremely difficult to defend.

Let's go back to Alan Sandage, for a moment. Remember, he was the scientist described by *The New York Times* as the grand old man of cosmology? He says,

> The big bang was a supernatural event that cannot be explained within the realm of physics as we know it. [108]

And returning to Steven Meyer from Cambridge, he says,

You can invoke neither time nor space nor matter nor energy nor the laws of nature to explain the origin of the universe. General relativity points to the need for a cause that transcends those domains. And theism affirms the existence of such an entity, namely God. In short, naturalism is on hard times in cosmology, the deeper you get into it, the harder it is to get rid of the God hypothesis. [109]

Taken together, the big bang and general relativity provide a scientific description of what Christians call creation *ex nihilo*, creation out of nothing.

As Nobel Prize winner Arno Penzias said about the big bang,

The best data we have are exactly what I would have predicted had I nothing to go on but the first five books of Moses, the Psalms, and the Bible as a whole. [110]

A FLY IN THE SOUP

Now, let's take a look at what we know about the origin of life on this planet. How did life arise from nothing?

In Genesis 1:20-25, God said "let the earth sprout vegetation and plants yielding seed." And, then, the Bible says the earth brought forth vegetation. As you keep reading in the first chapter, God did the same with fish in the ocean and birds in the air. He talked about living creatures on earth, and God spoke and it came into being. He brought into existence something out of nothing.

Up until the 1970s, maybe even the 1980s, the prevailing belief in science stemming from Darwin's landmark work was that if you were to go back to the primeval beginnings of the earth, you would find it covered with countless pools of water amid barren and rocky expanses, chemically enriched with the "necessary ingredients" to create life. These small bodies of water and their ingredients are referred to as "the primordial soup," and, as the theory goes, the earth at that time was an intense environment of constant electrical activity. Lightning would, of course, regularly strike this soup, at which point various amino acids, the building blocks of life, would be formed. Once these amino acids were formed, natural selection somehow takes over and life begins to evolve. Millions of years later, here we are, building computers and flying all over the world in airplanes. This theory really took off in 1953 when a scientist named Stanley Miller demonstrated, in the laboratory, how this could actually happen.

Miller created a pool of chemicals, the "necessary ingredients" to create an amino acid. He then pumped electrical charges into it and amino acids were formed. As you can imagine, Darwinian scientists were elated because if the origin of life can be explained solely through natural processes, then God is no longer necessary. [111]

Lee Strobel said that when he heard this taught in his high school biology class, it dramatically transformed his belief in God and led him to atheism. He said, "That's when I became an atheist." I, too, remember being taught this in my high school biology class.

Miller's experiment was hailed as a major breakthrough in science. Carl Sagan believed it was one of the most significant things that happened in man's quest for knowledge because it proved that life could arise on other planets.

The only way for Miller's experiment to work, however, is that the atmosphere of the earth had to be a hydrogen rich mixture of methane, ammonia, and water vapor. The only problem with this theory is there is no real evidence for such an atmosphere. Still there were those who believed the theory was sound because the experiment did produce amino acids.[112]

Then in the 1980s, NASA scientists actually demonstrated that the primitive earth had little if any volume of methane, ammonia, or hydrogen. Instead, the atmosphere at that time was composed of water, carbon dioxide, and nitrogen. This new information blew Miller's theory right out of the water. Miller's experiment, a theory on the origins of life, which had been taught for years as an indisputable scientific fact, imploded. And twenty-first century science doesn't, in fact, have any indisputable evidence on how life began on earth. Miller admtted in the periodical *Scientific American* nearly forty years after his famous experiment, [113]

> The problem of the origin of life has turned out to be much more difficult than I, and most other people, envisioned.[114]

Klaus Dose, a biochemist who is considered by the academy as being at the highest level of expertise on the origin of life says,

> More than thirty years of experimentation on the origin of life in the fields of chemical and molecular evolution, have led to a "better perception of the immensity of the problem of the origin of life on earth rather than to its solution. At

present, all discussions on principal theories and experiments in the field, either end in stalemate or in a confession of ignorance." [115]

In fact, Nobel Prize winning scientist Francis Crick, who, along with Stanley Watson and Maurice Wilkins, discovered the molecular structure of DNA, says,

> Every time I write a paper on the origin of life, I swear I will never write another one because there is too much speculation running after too few facts. [116]

Then Crick continues—and bear in mind he was antagonistic towards *any* belief in God whatsoever,

> The origin of life appears to be almost a miracle . . . So many are the conditions which would have to be satisfied to get it going. [117]

Allan Sandage, who we discussed earlier, who was honored in the astronomical field for having established the most reasonable and accurate estimation for the Hubble constant and the age of the universe and for which he won the National Medal of Science, concluded that God is,

> . . . the explanation for the miracle of existence.[118]

Dr. John Lennox is a Professor of Mathematics at the University of Oxford, a Fellow in Mathematics and Philosophy of Science, and a Pastoral Advisor at Green Templeton, Oxford. He is an author and popular lecturer on the interface between science, philosophy, and theology. He has participated in a number of debates with atheists Richard Dawkins and Christopher Hitchens, all of which were sponsored by the Fixed Point Foundation and moderated by author Larry Taunton.

Lennox relates a fascinating story about a brilliant scientist in England, a man by the name of Andrew Parker who is the director of research at the Natural History Museum in London. He holds professorships in a Chinese university as well as an Australian university. Lennox said he has known him for a number of years and that he is an expert in "bioluminescence," a field which studies the production and emission of light by living organisms. Specifically, Parker studies marine life that emits light, and, in his research, he came to the conclusion that the eye has played a central role in evolutionary biology.

One day Parker was giving a lecture on the subject of bioluminescence and a reporter in the back of the room raised his hand and said, "Sir, you sound like Genesis."

Parker asked, "What do you mean? Genesis what?"

The reporter answered, "You sound like Genesis in the Bible . . . Let there be light."

Lennox said his friend had never read the Bible and so he bought one and started to read it. And he couldn't let go of it. It astounded him.

Night after night Parker would read the first chapter of the Bible, Genesis 1. Dr. Lennox said Parker finally contacted him because he knew Lennox was a Christian and would therefore be interested in these things. Parker said, even though he was not religious, he would like to talk with him about science and religion.

The net result? Parker published a book called *The Genesis Enigma: Why the First Book of the Bible is Scientifically Accurate.*

Parker leads off with a caveat and then continues with the argument,

> I'm not a religious man and I do not want religion particularly at this time in my life. But what I have discovered is the most remarkable correlation between the order of events as I see them in the history of life and what Genesis says. There's no way the Hebrew writer of Genesis could have known that light was important, that marine life was important.

And then Parker goes through a whole list of points, facts as he knew them to be as a scientist, and then he concludes,

> . . . the writer of Genesis has it all in the right order. Could this be the evidence of God?[119]

Lennox says as brilliant as this book is it has been rejected by academics primarily because it is so unusual for a scientist who is not a religious man to be so forthright in correlating science to the book of Genesis.

FIRST MAN, FIRST WOMAN

The origin of man is probably the most controversial topic among Christians and their opposition when it comes to establishing the validity of the Bible. Genesis 1:27 says, "God created man in his own image," and in the second chapter, he forms man out of the dust of the ground.

You also see God's ability to create through the life of Jesus. For example, Christ transforms water into wine at a wedding celebration. He takes a couple of fish and loaves of bread and creates enough food to feed more than five thousand people. And then he approaches a man, Lazarus, who had been dead for four days, his corpse decaying, and he breathes life into him by saying, "come forward out of the grave."

Now when we turn to modern science's view on man's first appearance on earth, we get a very different explanation. It's explained by Darwin's theory of evolution, and it's important to know there are two types of evolution.

First, there's microevolution—changes that take place within a species that has been observed to be true, as seen, for example, in dogs or cats. And, second, is macroevolution. This theory claims that all living creatures have a common ancestor and that natural selection brought forth the development of every one of the countless organisms we see in the modern world, all from a single life form. Charles Darwin, who first articulated this theory, says that life evolves slowly by accumulating slight, successively-favorable variations over thousands and thousands and thousands of years.

However, the problem with evolution as a science, as well as God's creation as a faith, is that we can't prove either using the scientific method. In other words, *neither* reality can be proven in the laboratory. Darwin, however, made it very clear that natural selection's role in the evolution of the species would have to be validated by the fossil record. Darwin understood that if the theory of evolution is indeed true, there must have been a significant number of intermediate links in the fossil record, which would tie all life forms together.

However, with great humility and integrity, Darwin ultimately had to acknowledge that there was no great fossil evidence that had yet been found during his lifetime. He believed, however, that future fossil discoveries would vindicate his theory. And a new branch of science, the forensic science of paleontology, developed the tools and the methods to study the fossil record as it was discovered and developed.

This pivotal term used by Darwin, "intermediate linkage," is what he believed would have to be found throughout the fossil record if the theory of evolution was to be validated. For instance, there would have to be intermediate forms between early man and the apes. If you put apes (or, more particularly, according to current theory, *chimpanzees*) on one side of the room and human beings (*Homo Sapiens*) on the other, then, between these two, there should be a direct intermediate linkage to an intermediate species, our remote ancestor) As children, we generically label this linkage a "cavemen," but in the science of anthropology we speak of pre-humans with such names as Neanderthal or Australopithecus, early primate species continually evolving, in stepped gradations, leading to Cro-Magnon man, the first early human.

But why are there no surviving pre-historic ancestors? We have apes and we have humans, but there are no living "intermediate linkages" alive today. And this same absence of intermediate linkages goes for other species, too. Where are they? Supposedly, having died out, they must be somewhere in the fossil record?

The truth is that human scientists have been searching for our pre-historic ancestors in the fossil record since the mid-1800s. The reasonable question to ask is, How are they doing?

Well, apparently, not that well.

Lee Strobel, whom I mentioned earlier and used as a resource, was drawn to atheism because of what he was taught in biology class in high school. He went on a two-year investigation for the truth of life and during his search, he remained a believer in Darwinian theory. However, as he progressed, he became deeply troubled by the lack of fossil evidence for the intermediate links between the varied species.

Here are some examples of the type of observations he encountered. This first one is from a college textbook on general paleontology,

> One of the most surprising negative results of paleontological research in the last century is that such transitional forms seem to be inordinately scarce. In Darwin's time, this could perhaps be ascribed to the incompleteness of the paleontological record and to the lack of knowledge. But with the enormous number of fossil species, which have been discovered since then, other causes, must be found for the almost complete absence of transitional forms. [120]

David Raup, the curator of the Field Museum of Natural History in Chicago said,

We are now about 150 years after Darwin and the knowledge of the fossil record has been greatly expanded. We now have a quarter of a million fossil species, but the situation hasn't changed much. We have even fewer examples of evolutionary transition than we had in Darwin's time. [121]

T.S. Kemp, an Oxford Zoologist, writes,

Paleontology, certainly as much as any other branch of biology, and perhaps more than most, is prone to speculation. This consists of ideas that cannot be falsified, because suitable methods for testing them are simply not available. [122]

And probably the most influential evolutionary biologist of the twentieth century, who died several years ago, Harvard's Steven J. Gould, says this,

. . . the extreme rarity of transitional forms in the fossil record, persists as the trade secret of paleontology. The evolutionary trees that adorn our textbooks have data only at the tips and nodes of their branches. The rest is inference, however reasonable, not the evidence of fossils . . . Darwin's argument that the geological record is extremely imperfect, still persists as the favored escape of most paleontologists from the embarrassment of a record that seems to show so little evidence of evolution. [123]

David B. Kitts, School of Geology and Geophysics, Department of the History of Science, University of Oklahoma, allows the following cautionary advice,

Despite the bright promise that paleontology provides a means of "seeing" evolution, it has presented some nasty difficulties for evolutionists the most notorious of which is the presence of "gaps" in the fossil record. Evolution requires intermediate forms between species and paleontology does not provide them. [124]

Gould and many others have abandoned Darwinism for a new theory of evolution called "punctuated equilibrium," which holds that evolutionary transitions occur rapidly and not slowly as Darwin insisted. And Gould says this is why modern humans have such little chance of finding our ancestor primates in the fossil record. These transitions are catastrophic in nature—volcanoes, asteroids, drought, floods—and they happen so quickly relative to a geologic span of time.

There is a huge division now among evolutionists: does the natural selection process happen slowly, incrementally, or does a cataclysmic event so disrupt the ecosystem that it wipes out huge numbers of life forms all at once? Let's return to the fossil record for a moment. I remember as a kid—and you probably have seen this, too—there was an illustration in the World Book Encyclopedia. On the far left was an ape-like creature, and, next to this creature, moving to the right, you would see a succession of other ape-looking creatures along a timeline. Finally, at the end of the timeline, you would see a human being.

This means of illustrating evolution was an innovation of the American Museum of Natural History. And the second pre-historic man in line, after the ape, is who they call Java man. You may have heard of Java man because he was the first human fossil discovered in 1891 by Dutch scientist Eugene Dubois. It was a huge discovery at the time as many believed this was the missing link between apes and humans.

It was many years later though that the true story was discovered. Java man merely consists of nothing more than a skullcap, a single femur or thighbone, and three teeth . . . and a great imagination on the part of Dubois. This is what Strobel has to say about Dubois's supposed discovery,

> As a youngster beginning to form my opinions about human evolution, I wasn't aware of what I have more recently discovered that Dubois' shoddy excavation would have disqualified the fossil from consideration by today's standards. Or that the femur bone didn't really belong with the skullcap. Or that the skullcap, according to prominent Cambridge University anatomist Sir Arthur Keith, was distinctly human and reflected a brain capacity well within the range of humans living today. Or, that 342-page scientific report from a fact-finding expedition of nineteen evolutionists demolished Dubois' claims and concluded that Java man played no part in human evolution. In short, Java man was not an ape-man as I'd been led to believe, but he was "a true member of the human family." [125]

He says this was a fact apparently lost on *Time Magazine*, which, as recently as 1994, treated Java man as a legitimate evolutionary ancestor.

And then there appears to be credible evidence of a striking, almost unbelievable level of fraud (or, as seen in the best light, incompetence) in the creation of the actual number and identification of the fossils themselves.

Our investigative science journalists need to focus on how representative is the fossil record in terms of numbers of complete sets of life forms, the actual count of bones and complete skeletons. How many full, complete human skeletons do we have? And how complete and accurate is the science when reconstructing various life forms simply from a few bones?

Most of us are not aware that an anthropologist might find a jawbone or a skull or some teeth, and then will reconstruct a skeleton of what they think it *would* look like. They rarely disclose the fact that their conclusion, which is usually presented via the media in the form of an artist's rendering, has been based solely, for example, on one small part of a skull and one femur and a few digits from the left hand. (This is like having a police sketch of a criminal on the loose . . . except in these cases we have actual eyewitnesses; or like a rendering of a murder victim from just one or two bone fragments . . . except in these cases the renderings are consistently problematic, questionable, and seldom lead to an actual identification.)

In 1985, Richard Leakey, the famous paleontologist was a guest on the "Dick Cavett Show." Leakey had with him some impressive looking human fossils. As they were talking about the fossils, Cavett continued to gently press Leakey about how many of the bones were actually found in the ground.

Well, Leakey finally admitted, actually just a small piece of bone was found and then he and his team of experts reconstructed the rest with plaster. Cavett was dumbfounded.

Naturally, whenever you read about these great fossil finds, you assume it's this well-preserved ancient human skeleton. British paleontologist, Henry Gee, who's the senior science writer for the prestigious *Nature Magazine* said this,

> The intervals of time that separate fossils are so huge, that we cannot say anything definite about their possible connection through ancestry and descent. [126]

Gee called each fossil an isolated point with no knowledgeable connection to any other given fossil, and they all float around in an overwhelming sea of gaps. In fact, he said,

. . . all the fossil evidence for human evolution between ten and five million years ago, several thousand generations of living creatures, can all be fitted into a small box.

The Wall Street Journal in October 2011 ran a book review titled "Bones that Tell a Tale," presenting some compelling information from *The Fossil Chronicles,* a book by Dean Falk. The reviewer, Brian Switek, suggests that seldom has the discovery of an ancient human fossil ever been announced without stirring immediate controversy. He says for more than 150 years, revelations of a new species of our prehistoric kin have sent scientists into a tizzy about the meaning of the news. In his book review, Switek informs us that only a short while before his review ran in the *Wall Street Journal,* another source, *Science Magazine,* had announced the existence of two million-year-old "human-like" fossils found in a South African cave, yet no one has yet to agree on how this "ancestor" of ours actually relates to us. And the article goes on to say that every time there's a new fossil discovery, there seems always to be a huge dispute over what it actually represents. The principal reason? The fossil find doesn't add up, consisting of maybe a little bone, a jaw, maybe a skull . . . and that's about it. [127]

SIMPLE MATH, COMPLEX REALITY

In an effort to get my hands around this whole issue of man's first appearance in the world and what science can teach us about human life—I undertook a study on the history of the population of the world. After my initial survey of the resources available to me, I turned to the Population Reference Bureau. They work in conjunction with the United Nations and have produced a chart that purports to be an estimated history of the human population.

In 2009, there were 6.7 billion people on earth. In 1974, there were 4 billion. In 1927, there were two billion, and in 1804, 1 billion. As we get down to around 1500, the report indicates that they cannot tell us much more—as this is just an estimate, it states that there were approximately 500 million people alive in the year 1500. [128]

Year	Population
1500	500,000
1804	1,000,000,000
1927	2,000,000,000
1974	4,000,000,000
2009	6,700,000,000

You can see this doubling take place. The concept of "doubling time" is the period of time required for a quantity to double in size or value. It can be used for such things as bacterial growth and population studies, compound interest and tumors. So, I decided to extrapolate backwards down the timeline. According to my estimate, it takes roughly twenty-eight doubling generations, as you go back in time, until you would eventually end up with just two people. That's it.

So, the question is, Who were these two people? There seem to be two options.

The first option? As the Bible says, Adam and Eve.

The second option? Two pre-human primates, male and female, who become the "Cro-Magnons," the first *homo sapiens*.

Those are the two options and both, to me at least, are . . . miraculous.

While I was researching this information, there was this caveat attached to the Population Bureau's study suggesting that the set of specific characteristics that define a human is "a matter of definition." It is open to debate over which members of early *homo sapiens* should be considered human. Even if the scientific community reached wide consensus regarding which characteristics distinguished human beings, it would merely be to pinpoint the time of their first appearance as the fossil record is simply too sparse.

Which raises, I think, the necessary question. When did the first Cro-Magnon man and woman go from being animals into two self-aware human beings? When did they become designed in the image of God? When did they go from being animals to human beings that have souls? And, more important, when did they develop consciousness, an awareness of their self, their individuality? Now, I've been somewhat ambivalent on this over the years, but I have by faith concluded that the first two humans on earth were indeed "Adam" and "Eve," whom God created as described in the book of Genesis.

However, there are a great number of men and women (such as the scientist Francis Collins) who believe that God created everything in the beginning and life has evolved into what we see in the world today. It's called theistic evolution, with God's presence invested in each new life, in every generation from the beginning of time. I don't believe this is the means God has chosen, but some Christians do. What we can all agree on, however, is that we exist and God stands behind our existence, and as human beings, we reflect his glory.

AN INTELLIGENT DESIGN

Several times in my research, I encountered a scientist named James Tour. He's a professor in the department of chemistry at the Center for Nanoscale Science and Technology at Rice University. He has a doctorate in organic chemistry from Purdue; he has done post-doctoral work at Stanford and at the University of Wisconsin. Tour is on the cutting edge of research in the molecular world. He has written more than 140 technical research articles and holds seventeen U.S. patents. He says this,

> I build molecules for a living . . . I can't begin to tell you how difficult that job is.

In a speech several years ago, he described something he realized as he probed deeper and deeper into the awe-aspiring wonders at the molecular level,

> I stand in awe of God because of what he has done through his creation . . . Only a rookie who knows nothing about science would say science takes away from faith. If you really study science, it will bring you closer to God.[129]

Wherever we reach, from the smallest particle to the largest galaxy, from the alpha to the omega, in the room where we are reading these very words to the great natural world outside, we will find, if we seek, the fingerprints of an intelligent designer. Generations of brilliant men and women from the dawn of time have been lead on this quest by the intimations of God in the details. The deep mysteries of life, of emotions, of love and death—all, perhaps, can be studied and broken down into smaller and smaller components by the scientific method, but in the process the inklings of a creative force should always surprise us with awe and wonder.

SIX

THE MORAL IMPERATIVE

*There is truth, and there is falsehood. There is good, and there is evil.
There is happiness, and there is misery. There is that which ennobles,
and there is that which demeans. There is that which puts you in
harmony with yourself, with others, with the universe, and with God,
and there is that which alienates you from yourself, and from the
world, and from God . . . The greatest error in modern times is the
confusion between these orders.*

> – Charles Malik
> Former Lebanese Ambassador to the United
> States and President of the United Nations
> General Assembly

IF IT FEELS RIGHT

Below are a few words from an op-ed piece from *The New York Times*
writer David Brooks. Brooks is a very respectful, intelligent man, and his
pieces in the *Times* are always, I think, balanced and responsible. He titles
this, "If It Feels Right."

During the summer of 2008, the imminent Notre Dame
sociologist Christian Smith led a research team that
conducted an in-depth interview with 230 young adults
from across America. The interviews were part of a larger
study that Smith, Kari Christoffersen, Hilary Davidson, and
Patricia Snell-Herzog, and others have been conducting on
the state of America's youth.

Smith and company asked about the young people's moral lives and the results are quite depressing. It's not so much that these young Americans are living lives of sin and debauchery, at least no more than you'd expect from 18—23 year olds, what's disheartening is how bad they are at thinking and talking about moral issues. The interviewers asked open-ended questions about right and wrong, moral dilemmas and the meaning of life. In the rambling answers which Smith and company recount in a new book, *Lost in Transition*, you see the young people groping to say anything sensible on these matters. But they just don't have the categories or vocabulary to do so.

When asked to describe a moral dilemma they had faced, two-thirds of the young people couldn't answer the question or described problems that are not moral at all, like whether they could afford to rent a certain apartment or whether they had enough quarters to feed the meter at the parking spot.

Not many of them had previously given much or any thought to many of the kinds of questions about morality that we asked, Smith and his co-authors write. When asked about wrong or evil, they could generally agree that rape and murder are wrong. But aside from these extreme cases, moral thinking didn't enter the picture, even when considering things like drunken driving, cheating in school, or cheating on a partner. "I don't really deal with right and wrong that often," is how one interviewee put it.

The default position, which most of them came back to again and again, is that moral choices are just a matter of individual taste. "It's personal", the respondents typically said. "It's up to the individual. Who am I to say what's right or what's wrong?"[130]

The one phrase that seems to stand out in my mind is "moral confusion." There seems to be a great deal of moral confusion in the world, and our younger generations are at risk.

WHERE LINES ARE DRAWN

This is another reason God has chosen the written word as his means of communication. It keeps us from moral confusion. All laws and doctrine, in order to be just and equitable, have to be objective and verifiable, without being overbroad or vague. Thus, laws must be recorded; they must be written down. This is how any complex and dynamic society maintains moral order and coherence.

This is where the Bible plays such a vital role in the health and welfare of our culture. It declares there is a divine moral order that governs life, and that God is the moral lawgiver. His moral law is revealed in the Bible. In essence, God is telling us how life should be lived. He has given us a moral compass so we don't get lost and a road map to avoid moral confusion.

In a key scene from a provocative movie that came out almost twenty years ago, "Grand Canyon," featuring Kevin Cline and Danny Glover, the main character, played by Kline, has been to a professional basketball game and veers off the crowded interstate to take a shortcut to get home. Unfortunately, in the process, he soon finds himself in a pretty rough area of town, lost. When he pulls to a stop, the Lexus he's driving, suddenly stalls.

He immediately calls a wrecker service and, while he's waiting, you see these teenage thug-looking guys come out of the shadows. They see what they've found and they're getting ready to . . . well, we don't know exactly, because right when they're going to do some serious damage Danny Glover comes to the rescue. Glover drives up in the wrecker, and, as he steps out to hook up the car, the teenage thugs begin to protest because here they have a guy at their mercy. He drives an expensive car, he's a well-dressed lawyer, and he appears to be someone who could be carrying a great deal of money. Glover takes the leader of the group aside and announces firmly,

> Man, the world ain't supposed to work like this. Maybe you don't know that, but this ain't the way it's supposed to be. I'm supposed to be able to do my job without asking you if I can. And that dude [referring to Kline] is supposed to be able to wait with his car without you ripping him off. Everything's supposed to be different than what it is here.

Life the way it's supposed to be. Danny Glover's character was referring to a type of moral behavior that we expect from human beings. There seems to be a right way to live.

Donald Miller in his wonderful book, *Blue Like Jazz*, shares this about one of his friends.

> I know someone who has twice cheated on his wife, whom I don't even know. He told me this over coffee because I was telling him how I thought, perhaps man was broken, how for man, doing good and moral things was like swimming upstream. He wondered if God had mysteriously told me about his infidelity. He squirmed a bit and then spoke to me as if I were a priest. He confessed everything. I told him I was sorry, that it sounded terrible. And it did sound terrible. His body was convulsed in guilt and self-hatred. He said he would lie down next to his wife at night feeling walls of concrete between their hearts. He had secrets. She tries to love him, but he knows he doesn't deserve it. He cannot accept her affection because she's loving a man who doesn't exist. He plays a role. He says he's an actor in his own home. Designed for good, my friend was sputtering and throwing smoke. The soul was not designed for this, I thought. We were supposed to be good, all of us.[131]

We were supposed to be good, but we're not. This isn't the way it's supposed to be.

The social sciences in the modern world, such as psychology and sociology, help us observe the human condition and describe the relationship between man and society. They attempt to explain how people operate. Morality, on the other hand, prescribes the way things ought to be, the way people ought to live.

C.S. Lewis says that just as physical life is governed by the law of gravity, human beings are governed by the moral law—the natural moral laws he calls them. The only difference he notes is that the individual has the right to obey or not to obey.

The Christian understanding is this: the world is designed a certain way and God imparts to each one of us the way things ought to be and the way we should then live. The Bible is, in fact, God's morality. It spells out absolute moral obligations. These absolute obligations are binding on all people, at all times, in all places.

Not only are these moral obligations outlined in the Bible, they are also found within each one of us. Every human being has an innate moral sense because we're designed in the image of God. It doesn't mean we necessarily follow it, but it is there nonetheless. Animals don't have this. They don't have a moral sense. They don't act on moral or immoral instincts or intuition. If my dog goes out and kills a squirrel, I don't say he's evil. He is a Golden Retriever and that's just what dogs do.

But it's different with us as humans. We have a moral sense within us. It has been given to us by the God who has designed us in his likeness.

C. S. Lewis speaks of this moral sense we have in his book, *Mere Christianity,*

> Whenever you find a man who says he does not believe in a real right and wrong, you'll find the same man going back on this a moment later. He may break his promise to you but if you try breaking one to him, he will be complaining, 'it's not fair', before you can say 'Jack Robinson'. A nation may say treaties don't matter, but then the next minute they spoil their case by saying that the particular treaty they want to break was an unfair one. But if treaties do not matter, and if there is no such thing as Right and Wrong, in other words, if there is no Law of Nature, what is the difference between a fair treaty and an unfair one? Have they not let the cat out of the bag and shown that whatever they say, they really know the Law of Nature just like anyone else. It seems, then, we are forced to believe in a real Right and Wrong. People may be sometimes mistaken about them just as people sometimes get their sums wrong, but they are not a matter of mere taste and opinion.[132]

They are absolute moral obligations. Now, based on what I see out in the world, much of our society seems to have problems with the moral law found in the Bible, and there appears to be primarily two different categories of people who challenge this morality. The first does not believe in morality itself because they don't believe in God. The second believes the morality of the Bible is old-fashioned and not relevant to modern society.

This first group thus believes as follows: *We don't believe in God, and since there is no God, there is no moral lawgiver.* And if there's no moral lawgiver, there's no universal absolute to follow. All values become relative. Richard Dawkins, the notorious atheist, takes this view,

> The universe we observe has precisely the properties we should expect if there is, at bottom, no purpose, no evil, and no good, nothing but pointless indifference.[133]

In other words, Dawkins is saying we live in a universe where there is no evil and there is no good. There is no God to stand behind morality; there is no moral lawgiver to dispense it.

The second group is a much larger group. They believe in God, they may even believe in Jesus, and at the very least they believe in a spiritual world. However, they dismiss the morality of the Bible because they see it as archaic and outdated. They do not believe in objective moral truth, something you submit to and is universally true. They see morality as subjective; it is something you discover for yourself. This is particularly true for this group as it relates to sexual conduct.

Peter Kreeft, the brilliant philosophy professor at Boston College, who has written over fifty books, says that people's

> "fear of permanent objective laws is amazingly selective. It always comes down to just one area." Sex . . . In my experience, students, like professors, bluff a lot, and do adroit intellectual dancing. But I would bet a wad of money that if only the sixth commandment were made optional, nearly all the hatred and fear of the Church would vanish.[134]

Kreeft is right. One of the primary reasons modern people do not accept the Bible and Christianity is because of its teaching on sexual conduct, which is passé and therefore irrelevant. Most of us are on a pleasure and happiness quest, not a truth and wisdom quest. We want to follow our hearts and desires. Blaise Pascal, though writing 350 years ago, captured the essence of the human condition. He said people almost invariably arrive at their beliefs not on the basis of what is true, but on the basis of what they find attractive. What many people fail to realize, however, is that God speaks clearly and says all his commandments are true (Psalm 119:151). These decrees are not arbitrary but correspond to reality and the way life is.

One of the greatest philosophers in the last century was Mortimer Adler. He was an atheist for almost eighty years, but eventually became a Christian. When pressed on why he had been so reluctant over the years to embrace Christianity, he said,

> That's a great gulf between the mind and the heart. I was on the edge of becoming a Christian several times, but didn't do it. I said that if one is born a Christian, one can be light-hearted about living up to Christianity, but if one converts

by a clear conscious act of will, one had better be prepared to live a truly Christian life. So you ask yourself, are you prepared to give up all your vices and the weaknesses of the flesh?[135]

If you don't believe that God determines what's moral and immoral, you will generally find yourself facing all types of moral confusion, like the young people in Dr. Smith's research cited by David Brooks. And the reason is because if you believe there is no basis for absolute right and wrong, then you also believe there must be no true good and evil. There is neither a "morality" nor an "immorality." You are then compelled to come up with your own moral code by which to live. You have to come up with something . . . and it promises to leave you uncertain and conflicted.

In other words, we are given the freedom to invent our own morality. But then our greatest challenge becomes how to differentiate between what is right and what is wrong? What will be our personal basis for what is moral and immoral?

Tim Keller says that so many of us base our moral convictions on "what I like," "what I want," or "what I feel." It seems a person's final authority today is his or her emotions. Follow your heart, follow your feelings, follow your desires, wherever they lead you.

This reminds me of a very famous debate that took place back in 1948 between the philosopher Bertrand Russell, who was a very outspoken atheist, and Father Frederick C. Copleston, a Jesuit priest. It was broadcast in England on the BBC. The topic discussed was the existence of God, and, as the debate progressed, the two men addressed the moral argument for the existence of God,

> Copleston: How do you distinguish between what's good and what's evil?
>
> Russell: I don't have any justification any more than I have when I distinguish between yellow and blue. What is my justification between yellow and blue? I can see they are different.
>
> Copleston: You distinguish between yellow and blue by seeing them, so you distinguish good and evil by what faculty?
>
> Russell: By my feelings. By what I feel.[136]

Russell clearly believed there was not a transcendent law that was given to help us make moral distinctions, because he believed there is no God. Therefore, ethical decisions should be made on one's feelings. The modern saying that best expresses this system of morality is, "If it feels good, you should do it." This approach to life, however, seems to offer a slippery slope that can easily lead us into the abyss.

Arguably, one of the most evil serial killers to ever live was Jeffrey Dahmer, not only because he killed so many innocent victims but also because he cannibalized those he had murdered. Shortly before his death, he gave an interview from prison that was aired on ABC News. This is what he said,

> When I was in high school, I found within myself the desire to torture animals. I did not believe in God, I did not believe we were here for a purpose. . . Given that I was not here for a purpose and I am going to die and that is the end of me, I could not find any sufficient reason to deny the satisfaction of my desires.

Then, he tells us that as he got older he eventually reached the point where torturing animals no longer satisfied him, saying, *"At that point, I decided I'll torture human beings."* Based on his view of life and morality, he plainly admitted, *"I could not think of a reason why I shouldn't given my view of reality."* [137]

Now I'm not suggesting all atheists end up being serial killers, but it is obvious there was a real moral confusion in Dahmer's life, which stemmed from his worldview. He followed his desires; he responded to and eventually came to trust his feelings.

The best way to truly understand how a godless worldview leads to moral confusion is to consider Nazi Germany. When Hitler came to power, a new brutal moral philosophy came to pass in Europe. Hitler's dream was to see the triumph of the strong over the weak. When Germany conquered Poland, Hitler said that the weak, who could be useful, would have to be enslaved and all others would be murdered. He believed the Poles should be treated as sub-humans, and he planned to kill all Germans with disabilities. Hitler made it clear that in order to see his dream realized, brutality would have to be cultivated as a virtue.

After the war, when the Nazis were on trial at Nuremberg, they defended themselves with an interesting argument. These were the exact words used by their lawyers,

Granted, our legal system [talking about Nazi Germany] is not the same as yours. Our fundamental values are not the same as yours and we simply made our legal system reflect our own cultural values . . . Our rule involved Aryan supremacy and we did not regard Jews as human beings on the same level as Aryans. . . . From our standpoint, then, Jews certainly did not deserve to benefit from the Aryan rights. . . . And the only reason that we find ourselves on trial here is that you won and we lost. [138]

ALL THINGS PERMISSIBLE

Do you see what happens when we are left to create our own morality? The Nazi regime believed that killing millions of innocent people was lawful under the value system they had established. Brutality was cultivated as a virtue. This is why Russian author Fyodor Dostoevsky's famous quote, although written in the mid-18th century, rings so true, even today. *"If there is no God, all things in life are permissible."*

At the Nuremberg trials in the 1940s, however, it's interesting to see the response of the Allied judges. The chief counsel for the United States at these trials, Robert Jackson, appealed to permanent, trans-cultural values. He said you have to look to a law beyond the law. A universal law. He said that a system of ethics must point beyond itself. It has to be transcendental and its basis cannot rest within the finite world. Otherwise, he asks, how could one in good faith say the Nazis were guilty of a crime?[139]

Dr. Arthur Leff, now deceased, was a brilliant professor at Yale Law School. Back in 1979, he published an article in the *Duke University Law Journal* titled, "Unspeakable Ethics, Unnatural Law." Today, it's considered a very important and prominent essay. It is uncertain what Leff believed about God, but what troubled him was that if there is no God, then there's no way that one can make any kind of case for human morality, particularly human rights. Here is a paraphrased summary of what he said,

You can say it is wrong for a majority to take advantage of any minority by force, but that is an opinion and not an argument. You can assert all sorts of things, but what you cannot do is say one point of view is morally right and all others are not. If someone says it is all right to enslave a minority, and you say no, it is wrong, who is to say your view of morality is right and theirs is wrong. Maybe it helps to frame it this way: if there is no God, who among us gets to impose their will on everyone else? Who gets to establish the moral laws that people are to follow? These questions are so intellectually troubling that you would think there would be more legal and ethical thinkers trying to come to grips with this. [140]

Leff's words suggest that if there *is* a God, then he would make the law for us to follow. We'd base our law on him. And this, by the way, is how Western Civilization was built, with Biblical truth as its foundation. We require a moral foundation on which to build a culture.

As T. S. Eliot penned many years ago,

> It is in Christianity that our arts have developed. It is in Christianity that the laws of Europe . . . have been rooted. [141]

In his well-documented book, *How Christianity Changed the World*, Alvin Schmidt shows how the moral, biblical worldview of Christianity has had such a powerful and positive influence on the world. Through the historical record, he demonstrates the following,

- The idea of human rights came straight from the Bible, as God places a high view of human life and its sanctity.
- Christianity greatly elevated and exalted the value of women. Christ raised the dignity, freedom, and rights of women to a level previously unknown in all other cultures in history.
- Where did the idea of philanthropy come from? European historian Carlton Hayes said, "From the wellsprings of Christian compassion our Western civilization has drawn its inspiration and its sense of duty for feeding the hungry, giving drink to the thirsty, looking after the homeless, clothing the naked, tending the sick, and visiting the prisoner.
- Biblical teaching was behind establishing hospitals, creating mental institutions, professionalizing medical nursing, and founding the Red Cross.
- Slavery was accepted by virtually every culture in history, as far back as anyone can remember.

It never occurred to anyone that it is wrong. But
the abolition of slavery and the rejection of racial
segregation go back to the earliest teachings of
Christianity. The great historian Will Durant
made it clear that Christianity was not a segregated
religion, "It offered itself without restriction to all
individuals, classes, and nations; it was not limited
to one people . . ."[142]

Returning to Leff's argument, his words also suggest that if there is no
God, then moral law has to be grounded in human opinion. So we must
ask, who gets to establish their human opinion as law so that everyone has
to obey it? Why should your view of morality have privilege over my view?
Ultimately, what you end up with is that those in power will make sure their
moral values prevail. That's what happened in Nazi Germany. But you see
how this view of life creates moral confusion? And it's so contradictory.
This is what bothered C.S. Lewis so much during his years as an atheist.

My life was full of contradictions . . . I was at this time living
like so many atheists, in a world of contradictions. [143]

Lewis realized that as an atheist he didn't believe in a moral law. He
could not believe in one because it did not exist. Yet he was appalled by the
terrible things he saw in the world and in himself. He saw that the universe
seemed to be so cruel and unjust, and yet he could not understand from
where his idea of justice and injustice came.

You see, once Lewis became a theist and later a Christian, he quickly
recognized the presence of an absolute moral law which had been handed
down to us by the God of the Bible, and in the process he realized evil was
no longer this meaningless word but rather a stark reality in life.

BLUE FOLDERS

Norman Geisler relates a great story that illustrates the moral confusion
in people's lives today and how one's life will, in fact, be full of contradictions
when absent a moral standard by which to live. Geisler tells a story of a
philosophy student in an upper-level philosophy course. The student writes
a research paper arguing that there is no God and, consequently, goes on to

argue there thus can be no objective or absolute moral principles. Judged by the paper's research, scholarship, and argumentation, most would have agreed it was easily an A paper but the professor wrote these words on his paper, "*F*... I do not like blue folders."

The student stormed into the professor's office waving his paper protesting, "This is not fair, this is totally unjust. Why should I be graded on the color of the folder? I should have been graded on the content of this paper, not the color of my folder." Once the professor settled the student down, he asked quietly, "Was this the paper that argued that on the basis of the Godless universe in which we live, there are no objective moral principles such as fairness and justice? Did you not argue that everything is a matter of one's subjective likes and dislikes?" The student finally acknowledged, "Well, yes."

The professor said, calmly and precisely, "I do not like blue folders. The grade shall remain an *F*."

He said at that moment, very abruptly, the face of that young man changed. It struck him that he really did believe in objective moral principles such as fairness, such as justice and injustice. Eventually the professor changed the grade and gave him an A, but, he said, the student left with a new understanding of the objective nature of morality. [144]

It's easy to proclaim that there is no God, but it's quite difficult to live consistently and honestly within the resulting moral framework. Now, hopefully, this makes some sense. We have to have a basis for morality. Our morals cannot be determined by feelings and opinions of a plurality of men. Otherwise, we'll become neurotic and morally confused, and we'll have a difficult time living with the worldview we profess to believe in. This is again why the Bible is so important. It gives to humanity a permanent absolute, transcendental law and since the Bible is considered to be the means by which God reveals himself to man, we can know what is truly right and wrong, what is good and evil, what is moral and immoral. And this is what gives moral meaning and dignity to our existence here in this life.

Peter Kreeft, who has the credentials to make a statement like this, says,

> No society has ever survived or will ever survive without morality and no morality has ever survived without a transcendent source. [145]

C.S. Lewis said it even more simply,

Unless we return to the crude and nursery-like belief in objective values, we will surely perish. [146]

Lewis and Kreeft are both saying we cannot live without moral boundaries. They both recognized that if we remove God's boundaries, it will eventually lead to the destruction of our society. Furthermore, if we don't believe nor grasp the fact that God has dispensed his divine moral law to the world, then the depravity of man, the sinfulness of man makes no sense. Therefore, the heart of the Christian message—the gospel message—becomes irrelevant and inconvenient. Unfortunately, this is what has happened in the lives of so many people in our world today. These poor souls for whom there is no moral certainty are bound to muddle through life without ever experiencing true liberty and peace, which is ultimately found in God's law.

LEWY AND COLES

In this chapter, I have argued that God has given us moral truth because he knows what we need in order to live a vibrant healthy life. He is like our doctor, who prescribes what we need for our bodies. He does not make up arbitrary suggestions, but tells us what to do to stay healthy. The doctor knows and understands the design of the body, if we fail to listen to him, we risk jeopardizing our health.

We do have a moral compass, a moral certainty, and through it, we have the means to address the confusion we see all around us. This has been found to be objectively true in the lives of two brilliant men through their research and in their subsequent responses to it.

First, there is Guenter Lewy. An author and political scientist, Lewy has been a faculty member at Columbia University, Smith College, and the University of Massachusetts. Back in the early 1990s, he set out to write a book on why America does not need religion. He saw so many of his conservative colleagues taking the position that religion is foundational to morality and social stability. He intended to prove they were wrong. In his own words, he intended "to make a defense of secular humanism and ethical relativism." He wanted to prove that they were "damned wrong."

After extensive research, the sheer weight of the evidence caused Lewy to change his mind. Instead, with academic integrity, he ended up writing his book, *Why America Needs Religion*, arguing that religion, particularly

Christianity, leads to lower rates of almost every social pathology—including crime, drug abuse, teenage pregnancy, and family breakdown. He clearly recognized the positive influence Christianity makes on people's attitudes and intentions. He saw unmistakably how it instills responsibility, moral integrity, compassion, and generosity.

Lewy concluded,

> Contrary to the expectation of the Enlightenment, freeing individual from the shackles of traditional religion does not result in their moral uplift. To the contrary, the evidence now shows clearly that no society has yet been successful in teaching morality without religion. [147]

Lewy makes a strong argument that biblical morality makes a difference when it is followed out in the real world. The only way to explain the outcome of his research is to recognize that when people's lives are lined up with the objective structure of God's moral law, they are happier and healthier.

Dr. Robert Coles is a very unusual man. He is a Pulitzer Prize winning author, having written more than eighty books. He is also a prominent child psychiatrist and a literature professor at Harvard. He teaches literature to business majors instead of psychiatry to medical students, and the reason he gives—"We have systems here to explain everything, except how to live."

Coles has spent his lifetime interviewing and listening to people. What has he learned about the human condition?

> Nothing I have discovered about the makeup of human beings contradicts in any way what I learn from the Hebrew prophets such as Isaiah, Jeremiah, and Amos, and from the book of Ecclesiastes, and from Jesus and the lives of those he touched. Anything I can say as a result of my research into human behavior is a mere footnote to those lives in the Old and New Testaments.
>
> I have known human beings who, in the face of unbearable daily stress, respond with resilience, even nobility. And I have known others who live in a comfortable, even luxurious environment and yet seem utterly lost. We have both sides in all of us, and that's what the Bible says, isn't it? [148]

Coles says he receives a great deal of criticism from those in his profession, because he speaks of human nature in terms of good and evil, light and darkness, self-destruction and redemption. He says, "They want some new theory, I suppose. But my research merely verifies what the Bible has said all along about human beings."

THE LIFE OF JESUS

*A repeated story in Christian history is of those who have
set out to prove the falsity of the way of Christ and wound up
being his followers. This is, in nearly every case, simply because
in their quest, they were forced to examine facts and to think
carefully about them. Therefore, as C.S. Lewis once pointed out,
a "young atheist" can't be too careful about what he reads and
must steadfastly protect his ignorance.*

> – Dallas Willard
> Author & Professor in the School of
> Philosophy at the University of Southern
> California

THE REALLY BIG QUESTION

As we have discussed, according to the Judeo-Christian faith, God
has chosen to reveal himself primarily by means of a permanent written
document called the Bible. As a just, wise, and omnipotent God, he
has deliberately chosen to surrender what would seem to be his greatest
advantage, the power to compel belief.

God has chosen not to overwhelm us or enslave us by his awesome
power. If we were forced to "love" him, it wouldn't be love. Instead, he has
provided the written word and he invites all people, on their own free will,
to come and seek him and his truth, which is laid out in the scriptures. But
this leads to a legitimate question—Even if one concedes that the Bible is

historically accurate and that it has not been altered as it has been passed down through the generations, how do we know it is a divine book? What makes it divine? What sets it apart from all other ancient history books or books on philosophy?

Christians believe the Bible is the divinely inspired word of God because Jesus validates it. Jesus confirms that God has chosen the written, recorded word as his primary means of communicating his thoughts and his will to mankind. Christ clearly puts his stamp of approval on the Old Testament. On ninety-two occasions, he supports a position by first saying, "It is written," and then he quotes from the Old Testament to prove the point. And the reason he did this is because he considered the Old Testament scriptures to be the written word of God and therefore the ultimate authority in life.

Jesus could have come along and said, "Don't accept the Old Testament scriptures." Or he could have pointed out errors that he saw in it. Instead, he confirmed the truth of the Old Testament.

Christ also appointed the apostles, who were witnesses to his life, ministry, and Resurrection. One of their primary roles was to record what they had seen and heard. Clearly as his representatives, the apostles were ordained to tell the story of Jesus and expound upon his teaching. Their writings are what eventually became known as the New Testament record. (To read more on how the specific books of the New Testament were chosen to be included in the canon, see Appendix III at the back of the book.)

So, the really big question is not simply "Is the Bible the word of God?" but rather "Is Jesus the son of God?" If he is indeed the son of God, then this would mean he has the authority to authenticate the scripture as God's truth. The Bible tells us that Christ came into the world in the flesh. In John 1:14, we learn that God became flesh and dwelt among us and we beheld his glory. In Hebrews 1:3 we learn,

> He is the radiance of God's glory, the exact representation of God's nature.

While being tried for blasphemy, Jesus stood before the High Priest and was asked, *"Are you the Christ? Are you the son of the most blessed one?"* He replied, matter-of-factly, in Mark 14:62,

> I am and you shall see the son of man sitting at the right hand of power and coming with the clouds of Heaven.

Either that statement, as incredible as it may sound, is true or it's false. There's really no other position you can take when somebody makes a claim like that.

If it's not true, if Jesus is not God in the flesh, then what are we to make of him? What are we to make of this historical person who led such an extraordinary life? History clearly indicates he was not a mythological figure. Was he just a great moral teacher? Was he a magician? Was he an illusionist?

On the other hand, if he was the Christ, the Messiah, the son of God, what would that mean? It would mean quite literally everything. It would mean his entrance into the world would be the turning point in history. It would mean his teaching about life, death, and eternity would be true. Furthermore, it would mean Jesus would have the authority and power to confirm that the Bible is the living word of God.

ROCK AND ROLL

French journalist, Michka Assayas, had a fascinating interview with rock superstar Bono of the rock group U2. Bono is quite a popular figure and is frequently in the news. Furthermore, he is a Christian, which seems to baffle the media. In the interview, Assayas asks the question,

> Christ has his rank among the world's great thinkers. But "Son of God," isn't that a little far-fetched?

Bono's response?

> No, it's not far-fetched to me. Look, the secular response to the Christ story always goes like this. He was a great prophet, obviously a very interesting guy, had a lot to say along the lines of other great prophets, be they Elijah, Mohammed, Buddha, or Confucius, but actually Christ doesn't allow you that. He doesn't let you off the hook. Christ says, No, I'm not saying I'm a teacher. Don't call me a teacher. I'm not saying I'm a prophet.

> I am saying I am the Messiah. I am saying I am God incarnate. And people say, No, no, please just be a prophet. A prophet we can take. You're a bit eccentric. We've had John

the Baptist eating locusts and wild honey, we can handle that. Please don't admit to the "M" word, the Messiah. Because, you know, we're going to have to crucify you.

And he goes, No, No, I know you're expecting me to come back with an army and set you free from these creeps, but actually I am the Messiah. At this point, everyone starts staring at their shoes and says, 'Oh My God, he's going to keep saying this.'

So, what you're left with this is either Christ was who he said he was, the Messiah, or a complete nut case. I mean, we're talking nutcase on the level of Charles Manson. I'm not joking here.

The idea that the entire course of civilization for over half of the globe could have its fate changed and turned upside down by a nut case.

And then Bono looked at the interviewer, and said,

For me, that's far-fetched.[149]

C.S. Lewis expresses something similar,

I am trying here to prevent anyone saying that early foolish thing that people often say about Him: "I'm ready to accept Jesus as a great moral teacher, but I don't accept His claim to be God." That is the one thing we must not say. A man who was merely a man and said the sort of things Jesus said would not be a great moral teacher. He would either be a lunatic—on a level with the man who says he is a poached egg—or else he would be the Devil of Hell. You must make your choice. Either this man was, and is, the Son of God: or else a madman or something worse. You can shut Him up for a fool, you can spit at Him and kill Him as a demon; or you can fall at His feet and call Him Lord and God. But let us not come with any patronizing nonsense about His being a great human teacher. He has not left that open to us. He did not intend to. [150]

And in another essay, Lewis says,

> We may note in passing that he was never regarded as a mere moral teacher. He did not produce that effect on any people who actually met him.

In other words, no one in Jesus' time would have thought to themselves, *"Wow, what a great teacher."* Lewis continues,

> He produced mainly three effects. Hatred, terror, or adoration. There was no trace of people expressing mild approval. [151]

Either they hated him, they were terrorized by him because of the unbelievable things he did, or they adored him. They recognized Him to be God.

And then Lewis says, in conclusion, you have two choices.

> You either have to accept or reject the story. [152]

In making wise decisions in life, a wise person will look at all the factors and evidence that relates to the issue and will then make a decision. Often, it is a faith decision, particularly if there is no scientific certainty to back up the choice you make. To make a decision about Jesus and his message, one must consider the historical evidence, and make a determination based on the strength of that evidence. If I were to go into a court of law, I would lay out four vital points to make the case that Christ is the son of God.

POINT I – THE IMPACT ON HISTORY

Consider how Jesus' simple and short life in one of the most desolate places in the Roman Empire, had such an impact on history. A famous author, the historian and novelist H.G. Wells, who wrote the prominent book, *The Outline of History,* as well as many others, says,

> The historian's test of an individual's greatness is "What did he leave to grow? Did he start men to thinking along fresh lines with a vigor that persisted after him?" [153]

What Wells is saying, in one sense, is that you can gauge the size of a ship by the size of its wake. Though Wells did not consider himself a Christian, he applied this same test to the life of Jesus by saying,

> By this test Jesus stands first. [154]

W. E. H. Lecky, a great nineteenth-century historian who put no stock in any kind of revealed truth or religion, wrote,

> The character of Jesus has not only been the highest pattern of virtue, but the strongest incentive to its practice, and has exerted so deep an influence, that it may be truly said, that the simple record of three short years of active life has done more to regenerate and to soften mankind, than all the disquisitions of philosophers and than all the exhortations of moralists. [155]

Author Henry G. Bosch has made this observation,

> Socrates taught for forty years, Plato for fifty, Aristotle for forty, and Jesus for only three. Yet the influence of Christ's three-year ministry infinitely transcends the impact left by the combined 130 years of teaching from these men who are among the greatest philosophers of all antiquity. Jesus painted no pictures, yet some of the finest paintings of Raphael, Michelangelo, and Leonardo da Vinci received their inspiration from him. Jesus wrote no poetry, but Dante, Milton, and scores of the world's greatest poets were inspired by him. Jesus composed no music, still Haydn, Handel, Beethoven, Bach, and Mendelssohn reached their highest perfection of melody in the hymns, symphonies, and oratorios they composed in his praise. Every sphere of human greatness has been enriched by this humble carpenter of Nazareth. [156]

World renowned historian and philosopher Will Durant wrote a classic book, *The Story of Philosophy*, that still is used in many a class as an introduction to philosophy. He is a Pulitzer Prize winning author but he is most well-known for an eleven-volume series that he and his wife Ariel wrote. They spent over thirty-five years on this massive work titled *The Story of Civilization*, and the Durants were not friends of the Christian faith. In this series, one of the volumes covers the history of the Roman Empire, and from it we learn that after Jesus' death the Christian religion was considered an enemy of Rome, and this hostility lasted for over 280 years.

In 312 A.D., the edict of Milan went into law legalizing Christianity, specifically Christian worship. In 381 A.D., under Constantine, Christianity became the official religion of the Roman Empire. Durant's observation of what happened in Rome during this period of time is quite astonishing,

> There is no greater drama in human record than the sight of a few Christians, scorned and oppressed by a succession of emperors, bearing all trials with a fierce tenacity, multiplying quietly, building order while their enemies generated chaos, fighting the sword with the word, brutality with hope, and at last defeating the strongest state that history has known. Caesar and Christ had met in the arena and Christ had won. [157]

Durant goes on to say,

> That a few simple men should in one generation have invented so powerful and appealing a personality, so lofty an ethic and so inspiring a vision of human brotherhood, would be a miracle far more incredible than any recorded in the Gospels. After two centuries of Higher Criticism the outlines of the life, character, and teaching of Christ, remain reasonably clear, and constitute the most fascinating feature in the history of Western man. [158]

POINT 2 – PROPHECY FULFILLED

In Luke 4:14, Luke, the historian, relates to us the story of Jesus, who had been teaching in the synagogues with great wisdom. News about him had begun to spread throughout the whole countryside. He then travels to his home in the small town of Nazareth.

It is evidently of great importance for Luke as a historian to describe the exact account of how Jesus announces his ministry. So, on a Sabbath, Jesus enters the synagogue in Nazareth, and, as was custom, stands up to read from the scriptures. It was common Jewish practice to ask people in the synagogue to read selections from the sacred scripture, the Tanakh, what we know today as the Old Testament. Jesus stood, unrolled the scroll and read from Isaiah 61,

> . . . the spirit of the Lord is on me because he has anointed

me to proclaim good news to the poor. He has sent me to proclaim freedom for the prisoners and recovery of sight for the blind, to set the oppressed free to proclaim the year of the Lord's favor.

He then rolled up the scroll, gave it back to the attendant, and sat down.

This text that Jesus reads in Isaiah is one of the key Messianic prophecies. The Old Testament, written over a thousand-year period before Jesus was born, contains numerous references to a coming Messiah. A deliverer.

Luke continues his narrative, telling us that no one in that synagogue could take their eyes off of this man Jesus, who then says to the audience,

Today this scripture is fulfilled in your hearing.

They were perplexed and turned to each other and said, "Isn't that Joseph's son?" They weren't even sure who he was! But, of course, Jesus had lived there all of his life. Now, all of a sudden, here is Joseph's son declaring that he is the Messiah.

The heart of the New Testament's teaching is that Jesus is indeed the Messiah whose coming had been foretold for centuries. The problem in Jesus' day is the would-be Messiah was expected to deliver them from the bondage of Rome when, in reality, he is asserting that he came to deliver them from their sinfulness. And all of the Messianic prophecies of the Old Testament are fulfilled in the life of Jesus.

In the book of Matthew (Matt. 5:17) Jesus makes a very significant statement about his life and purpose,

Do not think that I came to abolish the Old Testament law or the words of the prophets . . . I didn't come to abolish but to fulfill.

Again, there's that word "fulfill." In essence, Jesus was saying that he had no intention of getting rid of Old Testament laws and instruction. He was not threatening political or social unrest and he was not going to call into questions the tenets of the Jewish faith. Quite to the contrary, he had uttered the words that could only have come from the Messiah. "I came to fulfill" the words of the Old Testament prophets.

A great definition of the word "prophecy" is found in the book of Isaiah, chapter 46, verses 9-11,

Remember the former things long past for I am God and there is no other. I am God and there's no one like me . . . . Declaring the end from the beginning and from ancient times things which have not been done, saying my purpose will be established and I will accomplish all my good pleasure. Calling a bird of prey from the East, the man of my purpose from a far country, truly I have spoken, truly I will bring it to pass, I have planned it, surely I will do it.

God was revealing the fulfillment of his covenant with the Jewish nation in sacred scripture from the very beginning of time, telling the Jewish people exactly what was going to take place in the future. Through the prophets he continued to let them know what they could expect with certainty. And then he tells his chosen people, in what must surely have been one of his most significant declarations, look for the coming of the Messiah.

The coming of the Messiah is at the very heart of the Jewish faith and, not coincidentally, it is at the very heart of the Christian faith.

Listen to these opening lines in Paul's letter to the Romans. He says,

Paul, a bondservant of Christ, called as an apostle, set apart for the gospel of God, which he promised beforehand. He promised beforehand through his prophets and the Holy Scriptures, concerning his son, who was born of a descendant of David according to the flesh.

And then, again, in Luke 24, the resurrected Christ gives his final instructions to his apostles, some of the last words before his final departure,

These are my words which I spoke to you while I was still with you that all things which are written about me in the Law of Moses, the prophets and the Psalms must be fulfilled.

And then, it says he opened their minds to finally understand the scriptures, saying to them,

Thus, it is written that the Christ will suffer and rise again from the dead the third day . . . You are witnesses of these things.

We see the apostle Paul on several occasions when he would go into a new city—Acts 17, Acts 18, and Acts 19—he would go directly to the synagogue where the Jewish people were at worship, and, in describing it, Luke writes,

> He would reason with them from the scriptures, explaining and giving evidence that Jesus was the Christ, the Messiah.

The evidence that Paul presented to the world was powerful because the evidence was two-fold: first, there was the Resurrection, and, second, Jesus had fulfilled all the Messianic prophecies and Paul could point out these prophecies by quoting the verses from the Old Testament scriptures and demonstrate how Jesus had indeed "fulfilled" the prophecy.

This helps explain the early church's explosive growth. The message was so powerful then and that same message is valid today.

Philip Yancey says that for centuries the phrase, *"as predicted by the prophets"* was one of the most powerful influences on people coming to faith. Justin Martyr, who we discussed earlier, the well-known teacher and philosopher, credits his conversion to Christianity on the impression made on him by the Old Testament's predictive accuracy. [159]

The French mathematician Blaise Pascal said that the fulfilled Messianic prophecies played a major role in his coming to faith. These were words he uttered over three centuries ago,

> If a single man had written a book foretelling the time and manner of Jesus' coming, and Jesus had come in conformity with these prophecies, this would carry infinite weight . . . But there's much more here. There's a succession of men, over a period of four thousand years, coming consistently and invariably, one after the other, to foretell the same coming. There is an entire people proclaiming it, existing for four thousand years, to testify in a body to the certainty that they feel about it, from which they cannot be deflected by whatever threats and persecutions they may suffer. This is quite a different order of importance. [160]

And then Peter Kreeft, the prominent philosopher at Boston College, said,

> If you were to calculate the probability of any one person fulfilling, sheerly by chance, all of the Old Testament Messianic prophecies that Jesus fulfilled, it would be as

astronomical as winning the lottery every day for a century. Even if Jesus deliberately tried to fulfill the prophecies, no mere man could have the power to arrange the time, place, events, and circumstances of his birth or events after his death. [162]

WILLING TO LISTEN

Barry Leventhal, a young Jewish man, was on top of the world back in 1966. He was the offensive captain of the UCLA football team. In the pre-season, they were predicted to finish last in the Pacific Eight Conference. However the team stunned everyone by winning their conference championship and then went on to win the Rose Bowl. Not only was he the captain of the team, he was also the star of the Rose Bowl. This was the first Rose Bowl championship UCLA had ever won. Reflecting back on that period in his life, Leventhal recalled,

> My life was great . . . I was a hero, people loved me. My Jewish fraternity chose me as the National Athlete of the Year and I basked in the glory of it all. . . . But soon after that victory, my very best friend, Kent, came to me and said, Barry, I've become a Christian and, as my best friend, I just wanted you to know that . . . .I had no idea what Kent was talking about. I thought he'd always been a Christian.

However, Barry was intrigued by the change he began to notice in Kent's life. And so several weeks later, Kent introduced Barry to a man named Hal who was a campus minister. One day they were in the student lounge and began a discussion of the issue of the Messianic prophecies. At one point the conversation grew tense as Hal was showing Barry how the predictions of the Messiah taken directly from the Old Testament had been fulfilled by Jesus. Finally, Barry blurted out,

> "How could you do this?

> "Do what?" Hal asked.

> "Use a trick Bible," Barry charged. "You've got a trick Bible to fool the Jews."

Hal responded, "What do you mean by a trick Bible?"

Barry said, "You Christians took those so-called Messianic predictions from your own New Testament and then rewrote them into your edition of the Old Testament in order to fool the Jews, but I guarantee you those Messianic prophecies are not in the Jewish Bible."

"Now, hold on Barry. Do you happen to have a copy of the Tanakh? Do you have your own copy?"

"Well, I've got one from my Bar Mitzvah. So what?"

Then Hal said, "I'm going to give you some verses. I want you to write them down and I want you to go read them in your own Tanakh and we'll just leave it at that."

The two men went back and forth, until finally Barry, wanting to get Hal off of his back, agreed to check them out. Barry hurriedly wrote down the references and then got up and left. He really had no desire to meet with Hal again.

However, Barry was intrigued by their conversation, and that night found his old Tanakh that he had not opened since he was thirteen. He was shocked at what he read. Every prophecy that Hal had given him was indeed in the Tanakh. He began to think the unthinkable, what if Jesus really is the Jewish Messiah? And if he really is the Messiah, what should he do?

He decided to keep silent about this for a while and concluded that he needed to do more research, particularly if he were ever to go public with his discovery. In his study, he was most intrigued by the suffering servant described by the prophet Isaiah, in the fifty third chapter. In Barry's own words, he says,

> I vividly remember the first time I seriously confronted Isaiah 53, or better still the first time it seriously confronted me," Barry explains. "Being rather confused over the identity of the servant in Isaiah 53, I went to my local rabbi and said to him, 'Rabbi, I have met some people at school who claim that the so-called Servant in Isaiah 53 is none other than Jesus of Nazareth. But I would like to know from you, who is the servant in Isaiah 53?'"

Barry was astonished at his response. The rabbi said, "Barry I must admit that as I read Isaiah 53, it does seem to be talking about Jesus, but since we Jews do not believe in Jesus, it can't be speaking about Jesus."

Barry didn't know a lot about formal logic at that point, but he knew enough to say to himself, that just doesn't sound kosher to me. Not only does the rabbi's so-called reasoning sound circular, it also sounds evasive and even fearful. Today Barry observes "There are none so deaf as those who do not want to hear.

"It was April now, more than three months after the glorious Rose Bowl victory. I suddenly realized that I had nothing that withstood the test of time, let alone the test of eternity," Barry recalls. "This was most graphically demonstrated to me by the Rose Bowl victory itself. Just a few mere months after the most significant event in my life . . . all the glory, everything involved, was now slowly fading away into a distant memory. Is that all there is to life?"

As he continued to study, as he continued to seek, he came to the conclusion that Jesus was the Messiah. And on the afternoon of April 24, 1966, Barry knelt down by his bed, humbled himself before God, acknowledging that Jesus was the Messiah of the world and that he needed God's forgiveness that came only through Christ. And he surrendered himself. He says,

There was no lightning or thunder, only God's personal presence and peace as Jesus has promised.

And since his remarkable discovery, Barry has been reaching the Jewish people with the truth that the Messiah has come. The evidence for this truth is in the Old Testament. And teaching others this evidence is the focus of Southern Evangelical seminary near Charlotte, North Carolina, where Barry currently serves as the academic dean and as a professor. [162]

A FEW AMONG MANY

There are a large number of Messianic prophecies that are recorded in the Old Testament which have been fulfilled by Jesus in the New Testament.

I will lay out a few of these Messianic prophecies to consider. (For a more comprehensive listing of the prophetic passages anticipating the fulfillment of the scriptural covenant in Jesus, see Appendix Two at the back of the book.)

ISAIAH 7:14

The book of Isaiah was written in approximately 700 B.C., seven hundred years before Christ. That would be like something today written back in the 1400s pointing to an event that would occur today.

> Therefore the Lord himself will give you a sign. Behold a virgin will be with child and bear a son and she will call his name Emmanuel [which means "God is with us"].

And the fulfillment of this prophecy you read in Matthew chapter 1, verses 18, 24 and 25, and then in Luke 1:26-35.

MICAH CHAPTER 5, VERSE 2.

Written between 740 and 690 B.C.

> But as for you, Bethlehem, too little to be among the clans of Judah, from you one will go forth for me to be ruler in Israel. His goings forth are from long ago, from the days of eternity.

The prophet Micah is describing a person who is eternal, who will come into the world and be born into Bethlehem.
And it's fulfilled in in Matthew 2:1 and Luke 2:4-7.

ISAIAH 9:6 (700 B.C.)

> For a child will be born to us, a son will be given to us, and the government will rest on his shoulders and his name will be called Wonderful Counselor, Mighty God, Eternal Father, Prince of Peace.

I find it to be of great significance that this child will be called "Mighty God." Isaiah's words are a foretelling of the Incarnation, that God was going to come into the world as a human being.
And it's fulfilled in Matthew 4:15-16.

ZECHARIAH 9:9 (520 B.C.)

Rejoice greatly O Daughter of Zion! Shout daughter of Jerusalem! See, your king comes to you; righteous and having salvation, gentle and riding on a donkey, on a colt, the foal of a donkey.

And it's fulfilled in Mark 11:1-10. Listen to what Tim Keller says in reference to this prophecy,

When Jesus rode into Jerusalem, people laid down their cloaks on the road in front of him and hailed him as a king coming in the name of the House of David. This type of parade was culturally appropriate in that era. A king would ride into town publicly and be hailed by cheering crowds, but Jesus deliberately departed from the script and did something very different. He didn't ride in on a powerful war horse the way a king would. He was mounted on an polos, that is, a colt or a small donkey. Here was Jesus Christ, the king of authoritative miraculous power, riding into town on a steed fit for a child or a hobbit. In this way, Jesus let it be known that he was the One prophesied in Zechariah, the great Messiah to come.[163]

ISAIAH CHAPTER 53

The most significant of all Messianic prophecies is found in Isaiah 53,

Who has believed our message and to whom has the arm of the Lord been revealed? For he grew up before him like a tender shoot, And like a root out of parched ground; He has no stately form or majesty that we should look upon him, Nor appearance that we should be attracted to him. He was despised and forsaken of men, A man of sorrows and acquainted with grief; Surely our griefs He himself bore, And our sorrows he carried; Yet we ourselves esteemed him stricken, smitten of God, and afflicted.

But he was pierced through for our transgressions, He was crushed for our iniquities; The chastening for our well-being fell upon him, And by his scourging we are healed. All of us like sheep have gone astray, Each of us has turned to his own way; But the Lord has caused the iniquity of us all to fall on him. He was oppressed and he was afflicted, yet He did not open his mouth; he was like a lamb that is led to the slaughter . . .

This phrase, the "lamb that is led to the slaughter" is describing Jesus before the Roman authorities. Jesus never said a word while they were crucifying him. He didn't even open his mouth.

They made his grave with the wicked, and with a rich man at his death . . .

We know he was crucified between two criminals and the wealthy Joseph of Arimathea buried him,

. . . because he had done no violence, nor was there any deceit in his mouth. But the Lord was pleased to crush him, putting him to grief; If he would render himself as a guilt offering, He will see his offspring, He will prolong his days, and the good pleasure of the LORD will prosper in his hand. As a result of the anguish of his soul, He will see it and be satisfied; by his knowledge the Righteous One, my servant, will justify the many, and he will bear their iniquities. Therefore, I will allot him a portion with the great, and he will divide the booty with the strong; because he poured out himself to death, and was numbered with the transgressors; yet he himself bore the sin of many, and interceded for the transgressors.

I remember speaking with a man named Baruch Maoz. He was from Boston. He grew up in the Jewish faith. Through a series of circumstances, similar to Barry Leventhal, he became a Christian and then later went to seminary and became senior pastor at one of the largest Christian churches in Israel.

I asked him this question, "How do the Jews today treat Isaiah 53? How do they deal with it? How do they explain it?"

And these were his words.

They treat it as if it did not exist . . . they completely ignore it.

One of the very fine pastors in our country today is a man by the name of Louis Lapides, a senior pastor at a church in California. He grew up in a

Jewish home in Newark, New Jersey, and his family attended a conservative Jewish synagogue. When he was seventeen, his parents divorced. He recalls,

> That really put a stake in any religious heart I may have had . . . On top of that, in Judaism I didn't feel as if I had a personal relationship with God. I had a lot of beautiful ceremonies and traditions but he was the distant and detached God of Mount Sinai who said 'Here are the rules, you live by them, you'll be okay, I'll see you later.'

And so, Lapides became a self-styled wonderer, what we would probably call a hippie, and ended up living in Greenwich Village in the 1960s. Eventually, he was drafted, and fought in the Vietnam War. He described it as a very dark period in his life,

> I witnessed suffering. I saw body bags; I saw the devastation from war. I was extremely bothered by all the evil that I had seen.

It caused Lapides to wonder, is there a God out there to explain all this? He had survived Vietnam and had safely returned stateside, however, the only way he could deal with the trauma of his war experience was by smoking marijuana and pursuing his interest in Buddhism. In fact, he aspired to be a priest, but while studying Buddhism, he found it to be so empty. It didn't make any sense to him, so he tried Scientology, then Hinduism . . . It was about this time he decided to change locations. He moved to California . . . and one day while out on Sunset Boulevard he encountered some Christians. He thought he would have some fun and heckle them a bit, since they were out preaching on the street to anyone who would listen . . . One of the Christians approached him and mentioned the name of Jesus. He tried to fend him off with his stock answer—"I'm Jewish, I can't believe in Jesus."

One of them, a pastor, spoke up,

> Do you know the prophecies about the Messiah?

Lapides was taken off guard,

> Prophecies? I've never heard of them.

The minister startled Lapides by referring to some of the Old Testament predictions. Wait a minute, Lapides thought; those are my Jewish scriptures he's quoting. How could Jesus be in there? When the pastor offered him a Bible, Lapides was skeptical.

"Is the New Testament in there?" he asked.

The pastor indicated that, yes, it was.

"OK, I'll read the Old Testament but I'm not going to open the other one."

Lapides was taken aback by the minister's response,

"Fine, just read the Old Testament, and ask the God of Abraham, Isaac, and Jacob, the God of Israel, to show you if Jesus is the Messiah. Because he is your Messiah. He came to the Jewish people initially and then he was also the Savior of the World."

To Lapides this was all brand new information. He'd never heard of this. It was intriguing. It was astonishing. So he went back to his apartment, he opened the Old Testament to the first book, Genesis, and he went hunting for Jesus among words that had been written hundreds of years before this carpenter of Nazareth had ever been born.

I was reading the Old Testament every day and seeing one prophecy after another. For instance, Deuteronomy talked about a prophet greater than Moses who will come and whom we should listen to. I thought, 'Who can be greater than Moses?' It sounded like the Messiah. Someone as great and as respected as Moses but a greater teacher and a greater authority. I grabbed a hold of that and went searching for it . . . for him.

As Lapides made his way, chapter by chapter, through the Bible, he says he was stopped cold when he read Isaiah 53. In the wake of the power of Isaiah 53, and after much time and study, he says he eventually encountered more than four dozen major prophecies in the Old Testament, which thrust him into a crucial decision,

"I decided to open the New Testament and just read the first page . . . With trepidation, I slowly turned to Matthew as I looked up to heaven waiting for the lightning bolt to strike." Matthew's initial words leaped off the page: "A record of the genealogy of Jesus, the son of David, the son of Abraham . . . " (Matt. 1:1)

Lapides' eyes widened as he recalled the moment he first read that sentence. I thought, wow, son of Abraham, son of David . . . It was all fitting together.

These fulfilled prophecies were very convincing to Lapides's intellect, until one day he finally concluded that Jesus was the Messiah and the New Testament gospel message was true. Yet it had not made its way from his head to his heart. He said not too long thereafter he and some of his friends went out on the Mojave Desert . . . most of them with the intent to take drugs. Lapides, however, wanted to use this time for reflection. As he spent time by himself out in the desert, he made this decision, and he prayed honestly and deeply,

> God, I've got to come to the end of this struggle. I have to know beyond a shadow of a doubt that Jesus is the Messiah. I need to know that you as the God of Israel want me to believe this.

And a while later, he says,

> The best I can put together out of that experience is that God objectively spoke to my heart. He convinced me experientially that he exists. And at that point, out in the desert in my heart, I said, God, I accept Jesus into my life. I don't understand what I'm supposed to do with him but I want him. I've pretty much made a mess of my life and I need you to change me.

And he said that God began to do that in a process that continues to this day,

> My friends knew I had changed and they couldn't understand it. They'd say something happened to you in the desert. You don't do drugs anymore. There's something different about you.

I would say, well, I can't explain what happened. All I know is that there is someone in my life and it's someone who's holy, who's righteous, who's a source of positive thoughts about life, and I just feel whole. [164]

Today, he's a senior pastor at a large church in California.

Over the years I have heard story after story of so many Jewish people, from all over the world, who have come to the Christian faith simply because of the convincing nature of these prophecies. You see men and women with deep intellectual and spiritual integrity who've chosen to look and seek the truth with open and honest hearts. These individuals have recognized, basically, that some of Jesus' last words to his disciples ring true,

> Everything must be fulfilled that is written about me in the law of Moses, the prophets, and the Psalms.

In my mind, this is one of the great proofs that not only confirms that Jesus was the Old Testament Messiah, but also validates that the Bible is the divine word of God.

POINT 3 – THE RESURRECTION

I remember a scholar of some note saying that if you are a person seeking spiritual truth, you should always start with Christianity. It is the only falsifiable religion in the world.

If you will recall, we said in the chapter on history that Christianity is the only world religion that makes spiritual truth depend on historical events. That assertion comes from the apostle Paul who said very explicitly if Christ is not raised from the dead, your faith is worthless, you're still in your sins, and Christians should be pitied for their foolishness.

The veracity of Christianity depends solely and completely on the truth or falsehood of a historical event, the Resurrection of Christ, and therefore it needs to be determined whether it is a historical event or not. Over the years, there has been many a skeptic who understood that Christianity is falsifiable. Therefore, you would think many disbelievers would set out on a course of research to prove that Jesus did not rise from the dead.

A number of years ago, I was working on a presentation that I entitled "Jesus, Divine or Mythological?" As I was doing the research, I began to notice just how many men had set out to debunk Jesus and Christianity. Through the study of the historical record they were convinced they could demonstrate how preposterous this clam of Resurrection really was. Yet, so many who set out on this journey, through their research, were eventually led to change their minds and become Christians.

Since I did that study that list has grown. J. D. Anderson, Lee Strobel, William Ramsay, Josh McDowell, Frank Morison, Gilbert West—each of them exceptionally reliable as a scholar.

I think the most intriguing of all these men is Frank Morison. A very gifted English lawyer, he set out to write a book that was going to be titled, *Disproving the Resurrection of Jesus*. He was convinced that he could prove what his title proclaimed. However, when he completed his research, he wrote a completely different book, now a classic, titled, *Who Moved the Stone?* Morison demonstrated that the rules of evidence in a court of law confirm Jesus' Resurrection. The opening words of the book are quite powerful,

> This study is in some ways so unusual and provocative that the writer thinks it desirable to state here very briefly how the book came to take its present form.

> In one sense it could have taken no other, for it is essentially a confession, the inner story of a man who originally set out to write one kind of book and found himself compelled by the sheer force of circumstances to write quite another.

> It is not that the facts themselves altered, for they are recorded imperishably in the monuments and in the pages of human history. But the interpretation to be put upon the facts underwent a change. Somehow the perspective shifted—not suddenly, as in a flash of insight or inspiration, but slowly, almost imperceptibly, by the very stubbornness of the facts themselves. [165]

Dr. Gary Habermas, a historian and philosopher of religion who is not only a prolific author but is also considered one of the foremost experts on the Resurrection of Christ has engineered the most comprehensive investigation ever performed on what modern scholars believe about the Resurrection. Habermas and a large team of researchers collected more than fourteen hundred of the most scholarly works on the Resurrection written from 1975 to 2003. They included in their study only the works that were most up-to-date.

Habermas says the works they studied come from across the ideological spectrum, whether they were ultra-liberals or what he called "Bible-thumping conservatives." He and his team collected all of this research and documented only the historical facts which they all could agree upon.

And this is what these scholars agreed took place,

AGREEMENT ONE

Jesus died by Roman crucifixion.

AGREEMENT TWO

Jesus was buried most likely in a private tomb.

AGREEMENT THREE

Soon afterwards, the disciples were discouraged, bereaved and despondent, having lost hope.

AGREEMENT FOUR

Jesus' tomb was found empty very soon after his interment.

AGREEMENT FIVE

The disciples had experiences they believed were actual appearances of the risen Jesus.

AGREEMENT SIX

Due to these experiences, the disciples' lives were thoroughly transformed. They were even willing to die for their belief.

AGREEMENT SEVEN

The proclamation of the Resurrection took place very early from the beginning of Church history.

AGREEMENT EIGHT

The disciples' public testimony and preaching of the Resurrection took place in the city of Jerusalem where Jesus had been crucified and very shortly after.

AGREEMENT NINE

The gospel message centered on the preaching of
the death and Resurrection of Jesus.

AGREEMENT TEN

Sunday was the primary day for
gathering and worshipping.

AGREEMENT ELEVEN

James, the brother of Jesus, and a skeptic before this
time, was converted when he also saw the risen Jesus.

AGREEMENT TWELVE

Just a few years later, Saul of Tarsus, Paul,
became a Christian believer due to the experience
that he also believed; that he thought was an
appearance of the risen Christ. [166]

As you consider this list of historical facts, number five is of particular
importance.

Habermas and all of these researchers agreed that the disciples had
experiences "they believed were actual appearances of the risen Jesus."
Notice their research did *not* conclude that Jesus had risen from the dead.
This is because clearly some scholars did not believe the Resurrection to
be a historical fact. This is not surprising. However, all fourteen hundred
of the scholarly works did agree, at a minimum, that "the disciples had
experiences they believed were actual appearances of the risen Christ."

Therefore, those who did not believe that Jesus had actually risen from
the dead could only conclude that the disciples were hallucinating or they
were lying. Keep this in mind as we examine agreements four and six in the
list.

Historical fact number four states that Jesus' tomb was found empty.
All agree there was a missing body and if Jesus did not rise from the dead
then one could only conclude that someone had to have stolen the body.
They also all agree in historical fact number six. The disciples' lives were
thoroughly transformed, so much so they were even willing to die for their
belief.

So, there's an empty tomb and the disciples' lives are transformed
radically. If these are considered historical facts, how does one account for

them? In relation to the empty tomb, if Jesus' body had been stolen, scholars agree you have three groups of people who would be motivated to steal it.

The Romans, the Jewish authorities, or the disciples.

The problem is that the Romans and the Jewish authorities are not very plausible suspects. Once the Resurrection was being proclaimed throughout Jerusalem, all they had to do was produce the body of Christ and Christianity would have died a very quick death. As the famous British historian Arnold Toynbee said,

> *If they only could have found the body of that Jew* [referring to Jesus] *Christianity crumbles into ruins.*

Toynbee seemed to be frustrated that they could not find the body.

And then you're left with the disciples. Could they have stolen the body, disposed of it, and then have spent the rest of their lives propagating a lie, particularly when the heart of their teaching was to be committed to proclaiming the truth? Does anyone seriously believe that these men who were discouraged, defeated, and who feared for their lives, would go out, steal Jesus' body and then proceed to boldly preach the Resurrection to hostile crowds? What would motivate them to do this? Why face prison, torture, and death, all the while knowing that Jesus' dead body lay in some hidden place?

A number of years ago, there was an article in the *U.S. News & World Report*, a prominent secular magazine, that was titled "Jesus' Last Days." It said, in part,

> Yet even the most skeptical Biblical scholars conceded that something extraordinary happened in Jerusalem after Good Friday to account for the radical change in the behavior of the disciples, who at Jesus' arrest had fled to their own homes in fear. Could Jesus' Resurrection account for the fact that within a few weeks they were boldly preaching their message to the very people who had sought to crush them?[167]

Historian Thomas Arnold, author of the distinguished three-volume work, *The History of Rome*, says this,

> I have been used for many years to study the histories of other times and to examine and weigh the evidence of those who have written about them, and I know of no one fact in

the history of mankind which is proved by better and fuller evidence of every sort to the understanding of a fair inquirer than the great sign which God has given us that Christ died and rose again from the dead.[168]

I have concluded that the many skeptics who set out to disprove the Resurrection only to change their minds did so because they found the evidence for it to be so compelling. They could find no other explanation to account for the empty tomb, the radical change in lives of the disciples, and the remarkable explosion of the early church—other than the fact that Jesus rose from the dead.

Warren Lightfoot, a former president of the American College of Trial Lawyers, draws from a number of reliable sources to make a truly brilliant and convincing argument in favor of the Resurrection, and it is included in its entirety in the Appendix One at the back of the book.

POINT – 4 IN ALL HUMILITY

The final evidence I'll present to you is quite powerful because it is so counterintuitive. Jesus did not impact the world through power, wealth, or by setting up a worldly kingdom. He did not employ any of the means that generally lead to greatness. Instead he chose the path of humility, which was clearly by God's design.

A worldly leader who was in a position to really understand and grasp this was a man like Napoleon. Read what he said right before he died,

> I die before my time and my body shall be given back to the earth and devoured by worms. What an abysmal gulf between my deep miseries and the eternal kingdom of Christ. I marvel that whereas the ambitious dreams of myself and of Alexander and of Caesar, should have vanished into thin air, and a Judean peasant, Jesus, should be able to stretch his hands across the centuries and control the destinies of men and nations." [169]

Think about what he is saying? Here are three famous men, Alexander the Great, Caesar, and me, Napoleon, seeking to control the world by power. When you see their lives contrasted with this one man Jesus, the humble carpenter, you have to marvel at how the world has been so powerfully impacted and changed through this simple life of humility. Napoleon goes on to say,

Time the great destroyer, powerless to extinguish this sacred flame, time can neither exhaust its strength nor put a limit to its range. This is it, which strikes me most. I have often thought of it. This it is which proves to me quite convincingly the divinity of Jesus Christ. [170]

Use your imagination for a minute. If God gave you the task of creating a life, any life, for your son or your daughter, that would enable them to have a huge influence on the world. What would you choose? Assume you can determine their giftedness, their achievements, their wealth. What would you choose? President of the United States? King of England? Chief Justice of the Supreme Court? Senator? President of Apple? A rock star, a movie star, an Academy Award winner, Heisman trophy winner? What would you choose?

Most of us would choose for them power and influence, some type of celebrity status, a mover and a shaker, a person of substance whose character, opinions, and actions extended deeply into in the world of commerce and politics.

I ask that because this is what God could have easily provided for Jesus. He could have put him in a wealthy Roman household, or in Athens, where all the scholarly influence resided.

God could have given Jesus every advantage you would want in life, but instead he was born and lived in the most desolate part of the Roman Empire called Palestine. He lived a very quiet life with his parents for thirty years as a carpenter. He left almost no traces of himself on earth, and he never owned any belongings or possessions that could be enshrined in a museum. He never wrote anything. He allowed himself to be taken into custody. He was mocked, beaten, spat upon, and, then, stripped naked in front of a massive crowd. He then was taken to the cross and was crucified between two criminals for all the world to see.

And he asked God the father to forgive those who executed him and then was buried in a tomb. Yet somehow Jesus and his small following have produced the dominant faith in Western civilization. *How do you explain this?*

Philip Yancey wrote in one of his books about the life of French philosopher and anthropologist Rene Girard, who was a very accomplished man. He ended his career as a distinguished professor at Stanford. At a certain point in his studies and research, Girard began to notice that a cavalcade of liberation movements from the abolition of slavery, women's suffrage, the Civil Rights movement, women's rights, minority rights, human rights, had gathered speed in the twentieth century. The trend mystified Girard because he found nothing comparable in his readings in ancient literature. Through his further research, Girard traced this phenomenon back to the historical figure of Jesus.

It struck Girard that Jesus' story cuts against the grain of every heroic story from its time. Indeed, Jesus chose poverty and disgrace. He spent his infancy as a refugee. He lived in a minority race under a harsh regime. He died as a prisoner. From the very beginning, Jesus took the side of the underdog, the poor, the oppressed, the sick, the marginalized. His crucifixion, Girard concluded, introduced a new plot to history. The victim becomes a hero by being a victim. Girard recognized that two thousand years later the reverberations from Christ's life have not stopped. And yet, ironically, at the center of the Christian faith, hangs a suffering Christ on the cross, dying in shame, for all the world to see.

And to the shock and consternation of his friends and secular colleagues, Girard announced that he had become a Christian because of the unexplainable life of Christ. [171]

EIGHT

THE HEART OF THE MATTER

*It is almost impossible to make [people] understand ...
that I recommend Christianity because I think it is objectively true.
But people today are simply not interested in whether a religion is
true or false, they only want to know if it will be comforting,
inspiring, or socially useful.*

– C.S. Lewis
Oxford Professor, Author

THE RELUCTANT BELIEVER

At the end of the day, when the evidence has been considered, we have to either accept or reject the message. To be more precise, we either have to accept or reject Jesus. This challenge was laid down by Christ himself when he said, "He who is not with me is against me." (Mathew 12:30, Luke 11:23) Furthermore, if we accept him as the son of God, we must accept the Bible as his divine message. What other alternative is there?

I remember a number of years ago I had several meetings with a lifelong friend. He had given a great deal of thoughtful consideration to the Christian faith and then came to this decision,

I believe what you have told me about Jesus is true, but at this time I think I will stay on the path that I am on.

Looking back on that conversation, I now realize that my friend was actually telling me that he believed the message to be true, but he rejected it. It was a polite and palatable way for him to renounce Jesus, and continue to live without God's interference.

From this conversation, and from so many other encounters I have had over the years, I have concluded that putting our faith in Christ is not so much an issue of the intellect as it is a matter of the heart. For so many people, it all comes down to how you intend to live your life. So many turn away because of what the Apostle Paul calls our "stubborn and unrepentant hearts." (Romans 2:5)

Whenever we face a decision that requires us to give up our autonomy, we will always find resistance in the heart. Our desire is to come to God on our own terms, but he does not give us that option. Jesus is a benevolent king, and when he rules in a person's life there is harmony. However as a king, we have the option to rebel against him and go our own way, or we can lay down our arms and serve him with our lives. These are the terms he has given us. "You are either with me or against me." There is no neutrality, there is no middle ground.

This is evident in the life of C.S. Lewis. As a skeptic, he was surprised that there were so many intelligent people, like his friend J. R. Tolkien, who not only believed in God, but that Jesus was the son of God. As Lewis began his spiritual search, he continued to gain new insights which were in conflict with his current beliefs. He then became aware of something that was quite significant. His intellect was taking him in a direction that his heart did not want to go. Lewis's mind was being drawn to what was true, but his heart was resistant. He later realized that his attraction to atheism was because he could gratify all the desires of his heart. He acknowledged that he had a strong desire in his heart to be free of any authority that might interfere with his life. To Lewis, Christ was "the great interferer."

Lewis had always sought to follow the truth wherever it would lead. He eventually came to the realization that his intellect had been satisfied. He acknowledged that Jesus was the son of God, and that Christianity was true. He then concluded that all that was left for him to do was to surrender his heart. He reasoned that God as God would expect nothing less than complete surrender. However, for Lewis this was not easy to do.

He realized that he was finally coming to a place of truth, only to find that the truth was a person, Jesus of Nazareth. He also understood he was not accepting a body of doctrine, but was submitting his life to a person, the person of Christ.

C. S. Lewis finally relinquished his will, because clearly in Christ he found the one person who could unify and guide his life. Furthermore, it became quite apparent to him, that Christianity was not a religion or a set of rules to follow, but was a relationship with God. A relationship that must be entered into with humility and a surrendered heart.

CHOOSING TO BELIEVE

I sometimes wonder how well we know ourselves, particularly the deep thoughts and intentions of the heart. I do not think we realize how feelings, desires, and emotions have such a great influence over the decisions and choices we make. They often will cause us to bypass our logic and reason, and lead us away from what is true. What I have concluded is that although our emotions and feelings may be real, they are unreliable.

As I work with people who are attempting to come to grips with the Christian faith, I often wonder what is going on in their inner most being. Are they being honest with me? Are they being honest with themselves? Are they being honest with God? Do they understand the tension that exists between the mind and the heart, and that this tension often paralyzes us and keeps us from following the truth?

One of the most wonderful examples that captures the essence of this human struggle to find Christ can be found in the life of Sheldon Vanauken. In his wonderful book, *A Severe Mercy*, Vanauken details his long spiritual journey. He first describes himself as an agnostic, but then later admits he was actually an easy going theist who regarded Christianity as sort of a fairy tale.

Though Vanauken lived in different places in the world, he somehow struck up a long distance friendship with C. S. Lewis. Much of the book is an exchange of letters between the two of them. In his letters, Vanauken would ask the spiritual questions that troubled him most, and Lewis would patiently and intelligently respond to them.

Vanauken then describes the spiritual breakthrough that brought him to faith. Please take note of his thought process and how honest he is with himself.

> Christianity—in a word, the divinity of Jesus—seemed probable to me. But there is a gap between the probable and proved. How was I to cross it? If I were to stake my whole life on the Risen Christ, I wanted proof. I wanted certainty. I wanted to see him eat a bit of fish. I wanted letters of fire

across the sky. I got none of these. And I continued to hang about on the edge of the gap.

At this point, he realized that he was in kind of a spiritual limbo. He described it in these words,

> The position was not, as I had been comfortably thinking all these months, merely a question of whether I was to accept the Messiah or not. It was a question of whether I was to accept him—or reject. My God! There was gap behind me, too. Perhaps the leap to acceptance was a horrifying gamble—but what of the leap to rejection? There might be no certainty that Christ was God—but, by God, there was no certainty that he was not. If I were to accept, I might and probably would face the thought through the years: "Perhaps, after all, it's a lie; I've been had!" But if I were to reject, I would certainly face the haunting, terrible thought: "Perhaps it's true—and I have rejected my God!"

> This was not to be borne. I could not reject Jesus. There was only one thing to do, once I had seen the gap behind me. I turned away from it and flung myself over the gap towards Jesus.

A few days later he wrote these words to C. S. Lewis—

> I choose to believe in the Father, Son, and Holy Ghost—in Christ, my lord and my God. Christianity has the ring, the feel, of unique truth. Of essential truth. By it, life is made full instead of empty, meaningful instead of meaningless. Cosmos becomes beautiful at the Centre, instead of chillingly ugly beneath the lovely pathos of spring. But the emptiness, the meaninglessness, and the ugliness can only be seen, I think, when one has glimpsed the fullness, the meaning, and the beauty. It is when heaven and hell have both been glimpsed that going back is impossible. But to go on seemed impossible, also. A glimpse is not a vision. A choice was necessary: and there is no certainty. One can only choose a side. So I—I now choose my side.

In describing his act of faith to his wife, Vanauken said:

> . . . dearling, I have chosen—the Christ! I choose to believe. [173]

The words of Vanauken that seem to be so pivotal are "A choice is necessary." He is correct, a choice is necessary.

This reminds me of my own journey when I reached the point where I knew I had to make a choice. For Christ or against him? I was afraid to become a Christian. I was afraid of how God would change my life. I wanted to play it safe, to be left alone to pursue the life I wanted.

At the same time, I was very ill at ease over the fact that I might be turning my back on the truth of life. As I recall, what caused me to waive the white flag and surrender was when I finally asked myself, what is the alternative? The alternative was to reject Christ's offer of the forgiveness of my sins, to reject his offer of eternal life, and to walk through life alone without him. Like Vanauken, I could not reject him. Therefore, one evening, I made the decision to surrender to Christ and put my faith in him. All I can say is that since that day, my life has not been the same. Walking through life with Christ has been the ultimate adventure, and I never dreamed that my life with him as my guide would have turned out so good.

TO WHOM SHALL WE TURN

"A choice is necessary." I learned the truth of this because you cannot remain neutral towards Jesus. To not make a decision, in the end, is to make the decision not to accept him. At a certain point in Jesus' ministry, he confronted his own disciples with the necessity of a choice. In the sixth chapter of John (vs. 66-69), many of his followers began to withdraw from him and chose to no longer follow him. They did not like what he was teaching. He is standing there, with only the twelve disciples remaining. He asks them "Do you not want to leave too and go with them?"

Peter responds and says:

> Lord, to whom shall we go? You have words of eternal life. We have believed and have come to know that you are the Holy One of God.

What a powerful response by Peter. If we do not put our faith in you, Jesus, who will we look to for eternal life? Who will we put our hope and faith in? This is the question we are all confronted with. It is the choice we have to make. If I do not look to Christ for eternal life, to whom shall I look? Who will I rely upon? Remember, faith must have a foundation, and if Jesus is not that foundation, who will be?

As I conclude this final chapter, I leave you with the words of Dr. Tim Keller. He boils down the choice we are faced with into simple and logical terms,

> If the claims of Christ are not true, then you should have nothing to do with him, for he is a wicked lunatic.

> But if he did rise from the dead, his claims are true. Therefore we should take everything in our lives and put them at his feet. We should build everything in our lives around him.

Everything.

APPENDIX ONE
RESURRECTION

THE RESURRECTION

Beyond A Reasonable Doubt and To A Moral Certainty

Warren Lightfoot
In Defense for the Truth of the Resurrection

I'm going to examine the evidence for Christ's bodily Resurrection and I'm going to analyze the evidence to see if it proves beyond a reasonable doubt, and to a moral certainty, that the Resurrection occurred.

First of all, the Christian faith depends on the Resurrection. Without it, we have nothing. Christianity stands or falls with Christ's Resurrection. Disprove it and you've disposed of Christianity.

In Paul's letter to the Corinthians, he says this, "If Christ has not been raised, your faith is in vain." And another time, "If Christ has not been raised, your faith is futile. Jesus himself stated it as his unassailable credential. Peter's first sermon at Pentecost focuses entirely on the Resurrection. If you take that principle theme out, there's no doctrine left in that sermon.

It's the cornerstone; it's the citadel of the faith. If it didn't occur, the power of death remains unbroken and with it, the effect of sin. If it didn't occur, we are left in our sins as we were before the world ever heard the name of Jesus. If it didn't occur, Jesus was not the Messiah. Without it, he was not shown to be divine. Without it, we have nothing.

But with it, we have everything. For me, the bodily Resurrection of Christ provides the answers to life's most fundamental questions. Does God Exist? We have the Resurrection. Does God care about us? Look at the Resurrection. Does God intervene? Consider the Resurrection. Is there life after death? The Resurrection is our answer. Was Christ who he said he was? He was resurrected. Does God promise and deliver salvation? Look to the Resurrection.

Christianity stands alone with its resurrected founder. The bones of Confucius, Mohammed, Buddha, and Abraham lie moldering in their graves. Only Christ's tomb is empty.

When we examine the evidence, I submit to you it's absolutely overwhelming to the point that any honest skeptic who looked at it could never remain a skeptic.

In fact, that very thing happened. A British barrister named Frank

Morison promised himself for years that one day he would sit down and write a book and he would disprove the Resurrection once and for all. But Frank Morison was an honest skeptic and he did a prodigious amount of research.

After hundreds of hours of analysis he found the Resurrection to be absolutely undeniable. The exact opposite conclusion he expected to reach. And he wrote the book *Who Moved the Stone*, one of the great evidentiary examinations of the Resurrection event. That book, together with Josh McDowell's *The New Evidence that Demands a Verdict*, influenced a lot of what I had to say.

One of Frank Morison's conclusions was this; the basis of Jesus' trial and conviction was that he predicted his Resurrection. So that's the beginning of our analysis. That Jesus himself foretold of his Resurrection.

The great British theologian, John Stott, who died a couple of years ago, pointed out that Jesus never once mentioned his death without saying that after three days, I'll rise again. The disciples couldn't understand it. They were confused; they were confounded by such a claim. In fact, they only understood it after it happened.

But there was a group of men who took that claim very seriously, and that was the Jewish leaders. They used that claim to bring Jesus down.

The Jewish authorities followed Christ everywhere. They listened to everything he said and they paid particular attention to such expressions of divinity. And for Jesus to repeatedly say that he would rise from the dead was, to them, the height of blasphemy. And consider what a pronouncement that was. What if one of us would say to ours friends that we expected to die shortly but after three days, we would physically rise from the dead. We would be regarded as a certified lunatic.

The Jewish leaders, though, regarded Jesus as someone infinitely dangerous to them. This Nazarene carpenter had already gathered hundreds of followers by his preaching, his teaching, and his wondrous deeds. Now he's saying he can overcome death. To them, that's sorcery.

Even more important, it's heresy and blasphemy, and those accusations are precisely what the Sanhedrin trial was based on. They used the same accusation that Jesus was claiming to be divine to justify taking him before Pilate, and there they changed the charge to treason. They accused him of placing himself above Caesar so that they could get the death penalty.

The disciples may not have understood what Jesus was claiming but make no mistake about it; the Jewish leadership knew exactly what he was saying. They knew what he was promising and they knew how important this was. Jesus deliberately states his claim of divinity on his proclamation that he would rise.

What is the evidence? We know more about Jesus' burial than that of any other person in all of ancient history. More than any Old Testament character. More than any King of Babylon, more than any philosopher of Greece, and more than any triumphant Caesar. We know who took him down from the cross and bore him to his tomb.

We know that the body was wrapped, and included in the wrapping was about a hundred pounds of spices to act as preservatives and those cloths and spices bind together in a cement-like wrapping.

We know where the tomb was. We know who owned it. Our sources for this information are Matthew, a disciple of Christ who was there when he was crucified; Mark, who some say wrote his account within 10 years of Christ's crucifixion; Luke, a companion of Paul and a great historian; and John, who was the last disciple to leave the cross, and with Peter, the first disciple to get there on Easter Sunday.

There was intense interest in Jesus' burial, not only by his followers, but especially on the part of the Jews and certainly on the part of the Romans. Everybody knew where that tomb was and it was this tomb that unmistakably and miraculously, on Easter morning, was empty.

But the one absolutely unassailable, indisputable fact of history is the empty tomb. It's a silent, immutable rock of evidence as we go through our analysis. From Easter Sunday on, there was this empty tomb.

Everybody knew where it was, a tomb owned by Joseph of Arimathea, and that it contained no corpse. And with Easter Sunday's event, the tomb passes from history. No one's concerned about it, no one writes about it. We have the extraordinary silence of antiquity about this tomb. There was no issue concerning it. There was no point in arguing about it because it was empty.

In ancient times, it didn't become a shrine; pilgrims didn't journey to see it, because it was empty. Christianity flourished right there in Jerusalem where one could walk over on one's lunch hour and look in the tomb for oneself. It flourished right there because the tomb was empty.

When the disciples began to preach the Resurrection in the middle of Jerusalem, the Jewish authorities would have produced a corpse in a heartbeat if they had it. They would have immediately produced it, and that would have trumped any claims that these Christians had. It would have ended the new faith right then and there. But they couldn't because the tomb was empty.

In their early sermons, Peter and the others place enormous emphasis on the Resurrection and they never once mentioned the tomb because it was empty. Even skeptics can't mount an argument to the contrary, so they moved to the next question and so do we.

How did it come to be empty? Either, on the one hand, by the act of humans, or on the other hand, by the act of God, by divine intervention; one or the other.

And let's look for evidence of human action. Let's go through the theories. There really four theories that some act of humans caused the tomb to be empty.

One that had been pretty much abandoned but that's been renewed in recent years by a Muslim sect called the Ahmadiyya. It is called the swoon theory. It holds that Jesus didn't die on the cross but merely became unconscious and later revived in the tomb and walked away.

There is not one iota of evidence to support it and we can cover it pretty quickly. Jesus was brutally whipped with a Roman cat-of-nine tails, a process during which many of the victims died; thereafter, nailed to the cross by his hands and feet so that he couldn't push up to take a breath. He couldn't aspirate with that excruciating pain in his hands and his feet.

And so there, on the cross, suffering from shock, exposure, loss of blood, and with his lungs filling with more fluid on each attempted breath, he died. That death was confirmed by the soldiers, whose job it was to recognize such things. It was reported to Pilate, and it was reconfirmed by thrusting a spear into his side, which pierced his lung. Taken down and wrapped tightly with grave clothes and spices, which acted as cement, placed in a cold tomb, without medical attention, food or water, for 36 hours.

These theorists would have us believe that such a victim could recover, get himself out of the cemented grave clothes, stand on his broken feet, move this massive stone that required several men, and thereafter appear a radiant and commanding presence on Easter morning. To me, that's not possible.

Furthermore, we are to believe that such a battered, tragic figure would look so well to his disciples that he could convince them that he'd overcome death. To me, that's not possible.

Then, he permits his followers to establish a faith based on his Resurrection, all the while knowing he was misleading them, and afterwards, he leaves and hides someplace for the rest of his days and watches the world transformed? Not possible for me.

Or, he takes his disciples into his confidence and he tells them that he didn't really die after all and together they conspire to foist a monumental lie on the rest of the world? They connive to perpetuate a fraud? To me, that's not possible and so much for the swoon theory.

Theory number two: the Jews stole the body. I don't really see any arguments in favor of this theory. The Jewish authorities, more than anybody would want to stamp out this new religion that threatened them. They would have produced the body as quickly as possible if they had it. They had neither the means; they couldn't get past the Roman guard, nor did they have the motivation.

It would be utterly against human nature for the Jewish hierarchy to steal the body because it would give credence to the Christian claims. In fact, they had gone to see Pilate and asked that he place a guard there to keep it from being stolen.

As we said, Christ's disciples didn't understand that Jesus said he would rise from the dead after three days, but the Jewish leadership certainly understood it. Ironically, the Jews, by insisting on the Roman guard, unintentionally provided positive evidence of the Resurrection. So, to me, it's not possible that the Jews stole the body.

Theory number three: the Romans stole the body. This one fails for the same reason that the previous one did—there's no motivation. It's utterly against human nature for the Romans to steal the body and keep it a secret and thereby assist the development of this new religion.

The Romans would have produced a corpse even more quickly than the Jews if they had one and stamp out these revolutionaries. It makes no sense and there's no evidence whatsoever to support such a theory. So, to me, that one's not possible.

Theory number four: the disciples stole the body—followers of Jesus stole it. Right off the bat, we have the matter of the Roman guard, and it was a Roman guard. When the Jews went to Pilate and asked for a guard, he said, "You have a guard", which is the imperative, "Here is your guard, go and make it secure." And this guard had ultimately to report to Pilate.

Many scholars believe that there were four Roman guards commanded by a centurion. They placed a huge boulder in front of the mouth of the tomb and secured it with a cord passing across the boulder and sealed each end with sealing clay. Anyone breaking that seal had to answer to Pilate.

Let's look at the passage in Matthew where the guards rushed to tell the Jewish priests that the body was missing. The chief priest gave them a large sum of money and told them to go report that, "His disciples came and stole the body while we slept."

Matthew reports they took the money and they spread the story as instructed. Saint Augustine had something to say about that concocted story, "Either they were asleep or awake. If they were awake, why should they suffer the body to be taken away? If they were asleep, how could they know the disciples took it away? How dare they say the disciples came and stole the body?"

To sleep on guard duty was punishable by death anyway, so the guards were in danger of being court-martialed. It is extremely unlikely they went back to their garrison and admitted sleeping on guard duty. They were subject to being court-martialed anyway because the seal was broken and the stone was moved.

So, there's no evidence that the disciples came anywhere close to that tomb until Peter and John got there early Sunday morning. And let's look again at what human nature tells us.

For the theory that the disciples stole it, one would have to believe that this utterly frightened and dejected group of peasants, sometime Saturday regained their composure and that they organized themselves into a strike force, and that they, capable of dealing with these four Roman soldiers and the massive stone, stole the body.

Human nature tells us they were terrified and incapable. Peter was their nominal leader. He displayed craven cowardice in the courtyard. The others had scattered. Not only were they worried about their own skins, they were totally disillusioned. Their leader had not proven to be the Messiah. A crucified Messiah is no Messiah at all.

He had not been what they had thought. He had not been divine after all. He couldn't even save himself when it came down to it. Nothing had turned out the way they hoped. They were in the utter depths of despair, defeated, despondent, and somehow, overnight these theorists would have us believe, they changed all that and became galvanized into brave action? For me, that's not possible.

But let's assume for the sake of argument that they could somehow transform themselves. What then? They go and do what seems to me to be the impossible. They confront the guard and the guard allows them to pass? That's not going to happen. Or the guard is asleep and doesn't wake up when they move the massive stone? And the guards remain asleep as the disciples go in and get the body and steal away into the night with the corpse?

And let's pause for just a minute to ask why the disciples would want to go do that. It's very clear from scripture they didn't understand Christ's third day rise again prediction until after it happened. So, why would they go, at great personal risk, to steal and hide the body?

But, let's continue with this theory. To believe this, one would have to accept that the disciples did it so they could found a new religion based on the vilest of lies. That these disciples in the days to come would risk their lives, and others, based on a fraud that they perpetuated.

Here's an important piece of evidence. Although the disciples were brought before the Sanhedrin because they were proclaiming their Master's Resurrection, those worthy members of the Sanhedrin never once charged them with the theft of the body, and, in fact, never mentioned that the body was stolen.

And we look again at human nature at this juncture. Following Easter morning and at Pentecost, the disciples began to change the world with their preaching. They preached a new religion and they devoted their lives to it and they faced insurmountable odds.

And those who theorized that the disciples took the body would have them basing everything they did on a colossal lie. Suffice it to say that the established religions were against them, the government was against them, and yet, they persevered. But these theorists would have us believe that they did so with the knowledge that they and their leader were frauds.

But, for now, these theorists ask us to believe that these disciples would risk death for themselves and for their fellow believers knowing that their entire underpinning was a lie. For me, that's not possible.

As John Stott says, hypocrites and martyrs are not made of the same stuff. Every one of these disciples except John died a martyr's death, we are told. That they'd do it to advance a monumental fraud is, for me, simply not possible.

And that's it. Those are the four theories. Those are the only possible explanations for human intervention. For the body to be missing because of what a person or persons did. That leaves us with the other alternative. Divine intervention. Resurrection. And let's look at the evidence to see if that's what happened. That Christ's body dematerialized and reappeared—the same body.

John describes in detail what he and Peter found at the tomb on Easter morning. You will recall they ran there after hearing the women say that the tomb was empty. John was younger and he got there first, but he wouldn't go in. And then Peter comes chugging up and together they go in, and they look at the grave clothes.

They saw all the grave clothes lying on the lower part of the ledge, together, but still wrapped, fold over fold, and none of the spices displaced.

The shape of the body was still apparent in the wrapped linens, but the body was missing. There was a gap where Jesus' neck had lain, and the head napkin is lying exactly where the head had lain, separate from the other clothes and it was not lying flat, but it was still in its twisted shape, rolled like a turban so as to encircle Jesus' head, but the head was missing.

John saw this and immediately believed that Christ had been resurrected. Peter, however, did not. Nor did the other disciples believe. The mere empty tomb was not enough for them, nor was the undisturbed but empty grave clothes.

Then we have the appearances of Christ post-Resurrection. First he appeared to Mary Magdalene, as she stood weeping outside the tomb. After Peter and John departed, she sees the risen Christ but doesn't recognize him until he speaks her name. Giving this incident further authenticity is this; in first century Judaism, a women's testimony was virtually worthless. Only on rare occasions would a woman even be permitted to speak in court. No one would invent a Resurrection story and have a woman be the first witness, just as no one would invent a story of an empty tomb and have women make the first initial discovery of it. The women's involvement simply adds authenticity to the evidence.

The next appearance was to Peter alone. Just the two of them, and what a great reunion that must have been. Peter reports this to the others and still, they are unsure. And then Jesus appears on the road to Emmaus and those believers rushed back to tell the eleven and still, they doubt.

Then Jesus materializes before them inside the locked room. There are ten of them. Thomas is not there and they understand the risen Christ stands before them, but not Thomas. When Thomas heard about it, he still doubted and he said he wouldn't believe until he placed his hands in the wounds from the nails and the spear. And then Christ appears to the eleven, including Thomas, and offers to let Thomas do just that, at which point Thomas falls to his knees and says, "My Lord and My God."

Then Christ appears to the seven beside the Lake of Tiberias. He shares a meal with them and conducts the poignant inquisition of Peter. "Peter, do you love me?" "Yes Lord." "Feed my Sheep." "Peter, do you love me?" "Yes Lord." "Feed my lambs." "Peter, do you love me?" And Peter is hurt by the repetition. "Lord, yes, you know I do." "Feed my sheep." Three times matching Peter's three denials, and we can see that Peter is being prepared for his great future undertaking.

There are other appearances. We are told by Paul writing in 56 A.D. that the risen Christ had appeared before at least 500 other people. Skeptics have to confront all these appearances, and the argument they advance is this—these people had hallucinations.

The theory fails, though, if you examine it from a neurological or psychiatric standpoint. Only certain kinds of people have hallucinations and those who saw the risen Christ don't fit that category. First of all, look at the disparity in moods. Mary Magdalene was weeping, Peter was wracked with guilt, Thomas was incredulous, the disciples were frightened, the Emmaus pair was distracted.

Neurobiologists tell us it's extremely rare that any two people would have the same hallucination, much less dozens, hundreds, at different times, at different places, under different conditions.

A skeptic arguing the hallucination theory would have us believe that these disciples and the other witnesses were subject to a high degree of mental weakness and emotional instability. Totally different to the character that they have displayed, as we will see.

The appearances were revealed by different senses, different human senses. They saw him, they heard him speak, they touched him, and they shared a meal with him. Luke reports Christ's words, "Handle me and see. For a spirit has not flesh and bones as you behold me having." They handed him a piece of broiled fish and he took it and ate it in front of them.

Here's another aspect of the evidence. People who have hallucinations are receptive to them. They want the hallucination to occur. Christ's appearances caused his followers to believe against their wills. Mary Magdalene thought he was the gardener. The disciples were frightened and thought he was a ghost. The travelers to Emmaus simply thought he was an uninformed stranger.

C.S. Lewis, with his brilliant logical mind says, "It's of crucial importance that on three separate occasions this hallucination wasn't immediately recognized as Christ. It would be as though God sent a holy hallucination," Lewis says, "but that he, the author of all faces, couldn't get the face on this one exactly right."

So the appearances were not precisely as Christ followers might have wished them. These were not hallucinations or wish fulfillments to emotionally unstable, gullible people. These disciples were tough, skeptical, hardy souls, slow to believe. Once they saw and heard and they touched, they believed, and based on that belief, went out and turned the world upside down.

No hallucination ever stimulated people to undertake work of great magnitude and while carrying it out, to lead lives of such rigid and consistent self-denial, suffering, or even death. No hallucination ever yet moved the world.

And that brings us to what John Stott says is the greatest evidence of the Resurrection. That's the transformation of the disciples. We return to the disciples, as we said earlier, for nine of them, not including John and Peter, the last time they saw Jesus was in Gethsemane.

What we have is this, a dejected little band of deserters huddled together and terrified that they may be the next to be arrested. The disciples were thoroughly disillusioned, a ragtag, clutch of despairing doubters. They had given up. Everything that they had hoped for had collapsed. Their Master had not been who he said he was. Instead of a divine Messiah, he was a crucified criminal, totally discredited, totally disgraced.

It was over and in their fear and their despondency, they had completely given up. That is the state of mind of these disciples when the sun came up on Sunday morning and it was from this condition of utter dejection that the resurrected Christ and the Holy Spirit produced the most profound metamorphosis the world has ever seen.

Once they saw and believed, they never doubted again. They never looked back. They went forward with a dedication that no resistance could stop, no persecution could silence, no punishment could alter and, as we noted earlier, the forces arrayed against them were enormous. Kingdoms and empires and governments criminalized their conduct. Every established religion opposed them and pursued them. They were hounded, tortured, and stoned to death solely because of what they believed.

Paul was a part of the great persecution that began in the first decade after Jesus' death and he participated when countless Christians were seized and put to death for their faith. Whole families were killed because they proclaimed Christ is risen. For these men to persevere in the face of such unrelenting adversity is solid evidence that Jesus rose from the dead and that the disciples knew that he did.

Here are three examples of such dedication. The first one is St. Paul. Paul, who was then known as Saul, began persecuting the Christians in 35 A.D. Everybody knew the tomb was empty, with the Christians saying that Jesus was raised and the Jews saying the disciples stole the body. Saul was a brilliant scholar, most likely a member of the Sanhedrin and he undertook with great enthusiasm this persecution, a violent persecution.

A systematic persecution, block by block, house by house, he rooted out the Christians and had them put to death. He was there when Stephen was put to death and was shocked by Stephen's serenity.

You see, Saul thought he was about the Lord's work. To him, the Christians were the essence of evil. They were heretics and blasphemers and they were corrupting the world with their dangerous and heretical messages. If it was humanly possible, Saul was determined to stamp them out. There was probably another aspect that added to Saul's violent hatred for the Christians and that had to do with the empty tomb.

There it sat, with the Christians claiming the body was raised and the Jewish leaders claiming it had been stolen. Saul came into this controversy on the side of the priest and he had to share their views about the disciples' theft of the corpse. Therefore, in Saul's mind, the Christians weren't just heretics threatening established faith, but they were doing so by being deliberate frauds, having secretly moved the body somewhere.

This aspect only added to Saul's fury and ruthless determination to eradicate every one of them. Saul hears the Christians are gaining a foothold in Damascus and he heads right there. We may not know exactly what happened on the road to Damascus, but we know that Saul perceived the risen Christ with at least two of his senses—sight and hearing.

And we know, from that moment on, Paul was a changed man. As we read in Acts, Christ appeared to Paul at least two other times. Consider the position that his conversion placed Paul in. Suddenly, he had become an enemy of his old colleagues, the Jewish leadership, and the great persecution then began to apply to him. At the same time, his former targets, the Christians, wanted no part of Paul. Literally, he stood alone. We read how the Christians came to be terrified of Paul. They refused to believe their old brutal implacable enemy had changed.

But changed he had and the years he spent in solitude coupled with the time he spent with Peter and James in Jerusalem produced the brilliant missionary we're so familiar and indebted to.

In his preaching, Paul over and over says that the underpinning of his faith is that Jesus Christ was raised from the dead. Through all his trials, tribulations, arrests, imprisonment, persecution, and death, Paul never wavered and his life, and his work, and his certitude are solid evidence of the Resurrection.

The second example is James the Just or James the brother of Jesus. Our earliest glimpses of James are given by Mark who records that when Jesus' ministry was just beginning, his family thought he was not in his right mind. They tried at one point to get him to discontinue his preaching, an urging that Jesus pointedly disregarded, saying, "Who is my mother and my brethren?" And he looked at those gathered around him and he said,

"Whosoever shall do the will of God, the same is my brother and sister and mother."

On another occasion, Jesus is preaching in the synagogue in Nazareth and Mark tells us Jesus' family was offended by his preaching, leading Jesus to say famously that a prophet is not without honor, save in his own country and among his own kin and in his own house. To say that James was a skeptic was to put it mildly and yet, the Resurrection changed James into the dominant figure of the Christian faith in Jerusalem. At least twice we hear Peter and Paul refer to him as just that.

From the position of apathy if not antipathy, James comes full circle to devout believer and courageous leader of the Christian faith. The Sanhedrin knew that about James. They knew he was the leader, and they knew if they could change James, if they could break James, they could cripple the new faith. So they hauled James before the Sanhedrin. They charged him with breaking the law by his preaching. James stood his ground and they had him stoned to death.

The third example is Simon Peter. We know so much about Peter and in his impulsive statements and conduct prior to Jesus' death, we find somebody we can identify with. In his inability to comprehend some of Jesus' words, we find even stronger affinity. We watch his bravery in Gethsemane and we're proud of Peter. After all, this is the man who said to Christ only a few hours earlier, "Lord I will never desert you. If I have to go to prison and to die with you, I will never let you down."

And so, in Gethsemane, we're not surprised to see Peter backing up his words and hacking off the ear of the high priest's slave. But Jesus heals the ear and allows himself to be taken away and bound. He tells Peter not to resist.

Still, we identify with Peter. He follows along behind and he gets another disciple, almost certainly John to get him entry into the high priest's courtyard, and then there, by the firelight, when the maid asks him if he's with the Galilean, Peter denies it three times, the third time shouting with a curse, "I tell you I don't know the man!" Then, we get a glimpse of Peter's innermost character and perhaps our own.

In the most important test he's ever faced, Peter fails miserably, just as we might have. And the cock crowed immediately, and as the bound Christ is led past the firelight, he turns and looks at Peter and their eyes meet and Peter flees weeping into the night. Peter has proved for all time that if the stakes are high enough and the danger is great enough, he is a coward.

We know nothing of Peter after that until Sunday morning. But human nature tells us that he was plunged into the blackest of despair. This is no leader. This is not Peter the rock; this trembling, fearful, wretched soul couldn't lead any movement. But after he peered into the tomb on Easter morning, Peter rushed back, no doubt to tell the others what he'd seen. He didn't yet believe, John tells us.

But then a remarkable thing happened. The risen Christ appeared to Peter when just when the two of them were there and we have two scriptural references for the wondrous reconciliation, and what a meeting it must have been, with Peter condemning himself over and over and with Jesus forgiving him over and over. It's only after that crucial meeting with Peter that Jesus goes before the other disciples in the upper room.

Here's what we do know about Peter. Beginning on Pentecost, Peter is a new and different man. He is completely changed. The coward of the courtyard is gone.

Standing in his stead is Peter the Rock who takes on the Jews, the Romans, and all who oppose the new faith. He thunders at the Jews, "You killed the Son of God and you must repent. You killed him, God raised him, and you must repent." Over and Over he accuses them to their faces. Utterly fearless, Peter has become the great Lion of God, leading the long march of the church as it changes the world forever.

Thrown into prison, threatened, persecuted, he's become the bravest of all in his pursuit of converts, and Jew and Gentile alike fall under Peter's sway and come to be believers. To me, there's no possible way for Peter to be transformed as he was other than by being in the presence of the risen Christ and the infusion of the Holy Spirit. To me, further irrefutable evidence of the Resurrection.

And there's more. We have the wonderful fourth gospel. John wrote the book with the other three gospels available to him. And he tells us why he wrote it; so that we will believe. John was there. When the storm was calmed, John was there. When Jesus was transfigured, when Lazarus was raised, on Palm Sunday, in the Upper Room, and at Gethsemane, John was there.

We recall that Peter trailed along behind the arresting party as they left Gethsemane with Jesus. When Peter got to the high priest's courtyard, he needed someone to vouch for him so he could regain entry. Scholars believe that someone was John.

John's father, Zebedee, was a successful fisherman, and his territory included Jerusalem, so because of that, John would be known to the high priest's staff. I believe that John was there when Peter was tested and failed.

I'm convinced that John stood there in the shadows and watched, trembling and mute himself. We know that after Christ was led out, he turned and looked at Peter, and Peter ran weeping into the night.

What about John? Isn't it likely that he trailed along behind the guards and that he was part of the large crowd watching Jesus' trial before Pilate? John must have been overcome as these events unfolded, racked with anguish and grief for his master, incredulous that this same crowd that only a week earlier had welcomed Jesus into Jerusalem were now incited by the Jewish leaders and were screaming at Pilate, "Crucify him! Crucify him! Free Barabbas! Crucify Jesus!"

We cannot imagine John's desolation as he watched Jesus being led to Golgotha. We do know this; of all the disciples, only John came to stand beneath the cross. And we know that the suffering, dying Christ asked John to treat Mary as his mother. John gives us detailed accounts of Jesus' death and its confirmation by the soldiers and his subsequent burial. We know nothing of John's whereabouts following Jesus' burial, but we can assume he was plunged into the same black despair that the other disciples were suffering.

And then on Sunday morning, we know that John was with Peter when Mary Magdalene ran to tell them the tomb was empty. When John saw the condition of the grave clothes, he immediately believed that Jesus was resurrected.

And years later at Ephesus, he sat down and either wrote or dictated his eyewitness testimony. By the time the fourth gospel was written, the church had become overwhelmingly Gentile so John is writing in a way that they can understand. John wanted them, and us, his readers, to know beyond a reasonable doubt, and to a moral certainty who Christ was and that he was raised from the dead. He gives us his moving and eloquent testimony so that we will believe, and he tells us that over and over.

He doesn't stop, though, just with the events he saw. He wants to be sure that we have it all in perspective. And so he writes a majestic prologue for us and for his early readers. His Gentile readers wouldn't know much about the Jewish traditions mentioned so often in the first three gospels, but one concept they understood, particularly the Greeks among them, was that of the divine logos. Logos, the mind of God.

Logos means "word" and it means "reason," and John wants to make it clear that the divine logos had come to earth in the form of Jesus. He wanted it be clear that this Jesus who had walked among them, Jesus who had been crucified, dead and buried, this Jesus who was resurrected from the dead, this Jesus had pre-existed the world. And so, John wrote his wondrous and mighty prologue.

And in those powerful words, we can understand the certainty of Christ's Resurrection and of our belief in it.

> In the beginning was the Word, and the Word was with God, and the Word was God. He was in the beginning with God. In him was life and the life was the light of all people. The light shines in the darkness and the darkness has not overcome it . . . The Word became flesh and dwelt among us, full of grace and truth and we beheld his glory. (John 1:1-5, 14)

Amen.

⇥ APPENDIX TWO ⇤
PROPHECIES

In his popular book *All the Messianic Prophecies of the Bible* Herbert Lockyer identifies three hundred Old Testament prophecies fulfilled by Jesus. If this is a topic of great interest to you, I highly recommend this well-documented book. Below you will find an abbreviated version of the Messianic prophecies fulfilled by Christ,

1. SON OF GOD

Prophecy—

"I will surely tell of the decree of the Lord: He said to Me, 'Thou art My Son, Today I have begotten Thee.' "

Psalms 2: 7 (Also see I Chronicles 17: 11-14; II Samuel 7: 12-16.)

Fulfillment—

"…And behold, a voice out of the heavens, saying, 'This is My beloved Son, in whom I am well-pleased.' "

Matthew 3:17 (Also see Matthew 16:16; Mark 9: 7; Luke 9: 35; 22: 70; Acts 13: 30-33; John 1: 34, 49.)

2. TRIBE OF JUDAH

Prophecy—

"The scepter shall not depart from Judah, Nor the ruler's staff from between his feet, Until Shiloh comes, And to him shall be the obedience of the peoples."

Genesis 49: 10 (Also see Micah 5: 2.)

Fulfillment—

"Jesus…the son of Judah…."

Luke 3: 23, 33 (Also see Matthew 1: 2 and Hebrews 7: 14.)

3. FAMILY LINE OF JESSE

Prophecy—

"Then a shoot will spring from the stem of Jesse, And a branch from his roots will bear fruit."

Isaiah 11: 1 (Also see Isaiah 11: 10.)

Fulfillment—

" Jesus…the son of Jesse…."

Luke 3: 23, 32 (Also see Matthew 1: 6.)

4. House of David

Prophecy—

" 'Behold, the days are coming.' declares the Lord, 'When I shall raise up for David a righteous Branch; And He will reign as king and act wisely And do justice and righteousness in the land.' "

Jeremiah 23: 5 (Also see II Samuel 7: 12-16; Psalms 132: 11.)

Fulfillment—

"Jesus...the son of David...."

Luke 3: 23, 31 (Also see Matthew 1: 1; 9: 27; 15: 22; 20: 30, 31; 21: 9, 15; 22: 41-46; Mark 9: 10; 10: 47, 48; Luke 18: 38, 39; Acts 13: 22, 23; Revelation 22: 16.)

5. HEROD KILLS CHILDREN

Prophecy—

"Thus says the Lord, 'A voice is heard in Ramah, Lamentation and bitter weeping. Rachel is weeping for her children; She refuses to be comforted for her children, Because they are no more.' "

Jeremiah 31: 15

Fulfillment—

"Then when Herod saw that he had been tricked by the magi, he became very enraged, and sent and slew all the male children who were in Bethlehem and in all its environs, from two years old and under, according to the time which he ascertained from the magi."

Matthew 2: 16

6. HIS PRE-EXISTENCE

Prophecy—

"But as for you, Bethlehem Ephrathah, Too little among to be among the clans of Judah,From you One will go forth for Me to be ruler in Israel. His goings forth are from long ago, From the days of eternity."

Micah 5: 2 (Also see Isaiah 9: 6, 7; 41: 4; 44: 6; 48: 12; Psalms 102: 25; Proverbs 8: 22, 23.)

Fulfillment—

"And He is before [or, has existed prior to] all things, and in Him all things hold together."

Colossians 1: 17 (Also see John 1: 1, 2; 8: 58; 17: 5, 24; Revelation 1: 17; 2: 8; 22: 13.)

7. HE SHALL BE CALLED LORD

Prophecy—

"The Lord says to my Lord: 'Sit at My right hand, Until I make Thine enemies a footstool for Thy feet.' "

Psalms 110: 1 (Also see Jeremiah 23: 6.)

Fulfillment—

"For today in the city of David there has been born for you a Savior, who is Christ the Lord."

Luke 2: 11

"He said to them, 'Then how does David in the Spirit call Him "Lord," saying, "The Lord said to my Lord, 'Sit at My right hand, until I put Thine enemies beneath Thy feet.' " If David then calls Him "Lord," how is He his son?' "

Matthew 22: 43-45

8. PRIEST

Prophecy—

"The Lord has sworn and will not change His mind, 'Thou art a priest forever according to the order of Melchizedek.' "

Psalms 110: 4

Fulfillment—

"Therefore, holy brethren, partakers of a heavenly calling, consider Jesus, the Apostle and High Priest of our confession."

Hebrews 3: 1

"So also Christ did not glorify Himself so as to become a high priest, but He who said to Him, 'Thou art My Son, today I have begotten Thee'; just as He says also in another passage, 'Thou art a priest forever according to the order of Melchizedek.' "

Hebrews 5: 5, 6

9. SPECIAL ANOINTMENT OF HOLY SPIRIT

Prophecy—

"And the Spirit of the Lord will rest on Him, The spirit of wisdom and under-standing, The spirit of counsel and strength, The spirit of knowledge and the fear of the Lord."

Isaiah 11: 2 (Also see Psalms 45: 7; Isaiah 42: 1; 61: 1, 2.)

Fulfillment—

"And after being baptized, Jesus went up immediately from the water ; and behold, the heavens were opened, and he saw the Spirit of God descending as a dove, and coming upon Him, and behold, a voice out of the heavens, saying, 'This is My beloved Son, in whom I am well-pleased.' "

Matthew 3: 16, 17 (Also see Matthew 12: 17-21; Mark 1: 10, 11; Luke 4: 15-21, 43; John 1: 32.)

10. PRECEDED BY MESSENGER

Prophecy—

"A voice is calling, 'Clear the way for the Lord in the wilderness; Make smooth in the desert a highway for our God.' "

Isaiah 40: 3 (Also see Malachi 3: 1.)

Fulfillment—

"…John the Baptist came, preaching in the wilderness of Judea, saying, 'Repent, for the kingdom of heaven is at hand.'"

Matthew 3: 1, 2 (Also see Matthew 3: 3; 11: 10; John 1: 23; Luke 1: 17.)

11. MINISTRY TO BEGIN IN GALILEE

Prophecy—

"But there will be no more gloom for her who was in anguish; in earlier times He treated the land of Zebulun and the land of Napthtali with contempt, but later on He shall make it glorious, by the way of the sea, on the other side of Jordan, Galilee of the Gentiles."

Isaiah 9: 1

Fulfillment—

"Now when He heard that John had been taken into custody, He withdrew into Galilee; and leaving Nazareth, He came and settled in Capernaum, which is by the sea, in the region of Zebulun and Napthtali. From that time Jesus began to preach and say, 'Repent, for the kingdom of heaven is at hand.' "

Matthew 4: 12, 13, 17

12. MINISTRY OF MIRACLES

Prophecy—

"Then the eyes of the blind will be opened, And the ears of the deaf will be unstopped. Then the lame will leap like a deer, And the tongue of the dumb will shout for joy."

Isaiah 35: 5, 6a (Also see Isaiah 32: 3, 4.)

Fulfillment—

"And Jesus was going about all the cities and the villages, teaching in their synagogues, and proclaiming the gospel of the kingdom, and healing every kind of disease and every kind of sickness."

Matthew 9: 35 (Also see Matthew 9: 32, 33; 11: 4-6; Mark 7: 33-35; John 5: 5-9; 9: 6-11; 11: 43, 44, 47.)

13. "STONE OF STUMBLING" TO JEWS

Prophecy—

"The stone which the builders rejected Has become the chief cornerstone."

Psalms 118: 22 (Also see Isaiah 8: 14; 28: 16.)

Fulfillment—

"This precious value, then, is for you who believe, but for those who disbelieve, 'the stone which the builders rejected, this became the very cornerstone.' "

I Peter 2: 7 (Also see Romans 9: 32, 33.)

14. RESURRECTION

Prophecy—

"For Thou wilt not abandon my soul to Sheol; Neither wilt Thou allow Thy Holy One to see the pit."

Psalms 16: 10 (Also see Psalms 30: 3; 41: 10; 118: 17; Hosea 6: 2.)

Fulfillment—

"…He was neither abandoned to Hades, nor did His flesh suffer decay."

Acts 2: 31 (Also see Acts 13: 33; Luke 24:46; Mark 16: 6; Matthew 28: 6.)

15. HANDS AND FEET PIERCED

Prophecy—

"…They pierced my hands and my feet."

Psalms 22: 16 (Also see Zechariah 12: 10.)

Fulfillment—

"And when they came to the place called the Skull, there they crucified Him…"

Luke 23: 33 (Also see John 20:25.)

16. GARMENTS PARTED AND LOTS CAST

Prophecy—

"They divide my garments among them, And for my clothing they cast lots."

Psalms 22: 18

Fulfillment—

"The soldiers therefore, when they had crucified Jesus, took His outer garments and made four parts, a part to every soldier and also the tunic; now the tunic was seamless, woven in one piece. They said… 'Let us not tear it, but cast lots for it, to decide whose it shall be….' "

John 19: 23, 24

17. HIS FORSAKEN CRY

Prophecy—

"My God, my God, why hast Thou forsaken me?"

Psalms 22: 1a

Fulfillment—

"And about the ninth hour Jesus cried out with a loud voice, saying, 'Eli, Eli lama sabachthani?' that is, 'My God, my God, why hast Thou forsaken Me?' "

Matthew 27: 46

18. DARKNESS OVER THE LAND

Prophecy—

" 'And it will come about in that day,' declares the Lord God, 'That I shall make the sun go down at noon And make the earth dark in broad daylight.' "

Amos 8: 9

Fulfillment—

"Now from the sixth hour darkness fell upon all the land until the ninth hour."

Matthew 27: 45

APPENDIX THREE
THE CANON

THE CANON: EYEWITNESS TO TRUTH

In the Old Testament in the book of Amos in Chapter 4, verse 13, we are told that God declared unto mankind his thoughts and these thoughts have been brought into our reach because they had been put into words.

Human speech that can be clearly understood, documented through the written word, is the model that God has chosen to reveal himself to us down through the ages.

In fact, in the Old Testament, we are told how God's written words came into being. In the opening sentences of Jeremiah's first chapter, we are told that these are the words of Jeremiah (Jeremiah 1:1), and then in v. 2 we are told that the Word of the Lord came to him.

As John Stott says,

> So Scripture is neither the Word of God only nor the words of men only, but the Word of God through the words of men . . . This is the double authorship of scripture to which we need to hold fast. [175]

As Peter himself described it, he said,

> God's word is not an act of human will but men moved by the Holy Spirit spoke from God.

So biblical truth is inspired truth . . . but it is also eyewitness truth. You see this in both the Old and the New Testaments. As Peter, making reference to the Transfiguration, says, *"We were eyewitnesses of his majesty."* And the apostles who authored and approved the New Testament books were eyewitnesses of the Risen Christ. In fact, that was required to be an apostle, and, again as John Stott says,

> . . . this eyewitness principle lies behind all scripture, for God raised up witnesses to record and interpret what he was doing in Israel. [176]

So with that being said, how was it determined which of the inspired books should be included in the Bible that we have today? This process of determining which books are chosen is called canonization and the word canon as applied to the Bible means an officially accepted list of books.

However, it is important to note that there is a difference in the

Catholic and Protestant Bibles. They both recognize the same books in the New Testament canon. It is in the Old Testament where you see clear differences.

The Old Testament is called the Tanakh by the Jewish people. It is called by some the Hebrew Bible. The Protestant Old Testament is the same as the Tanakh in content. The Roman Catholic Church recognizes seven additional books, based upon these books being present in a number of Greek translations of the Old Testament. Over the centuries, there has been a consistent disagreement over whether these were merely books of the church, or whether they should be considered books of the canon and therefore included in the Old Testament as the word of God.

THE OLD TESTAMENT

The Hebrew Bible, which the church inherited from the Jews, is divided into three sections. They call these three sections the law, the prophets, and the writings, and each of these sections covers one of three successive periods of history.

In the early books of the Old Testament, it had been recognized from ancient times that if God's revelation is to be preserved, it had to be written down. For instance, in Exodus 17:14, after Israel led by Joshua had defeated one of their enemies, and where God had clearly intervened to help them, God said to Moses,

> Write this on a scroll as something to be remembered.

In Deuteronomy 31:24, God speaks to Moses and tells him to write in a book the *"words of my law."* God then says to Isaiah (Isaiah 30:8)

> Now go write it on a tablet before them, and inscribe it on a scroll that it may serve in the time to come as a witness forever.

It becomes clear that God wanted certain historical events and spiritual truth written down and documented for the benefit of future generations.

It was his revelation—what he wanted recorded and these words were the basis of the covenant relationship between God and his people. And what you see over time is that Moses and Joshua will add God's writings to this book of the covenant. And then most scholars believe that the final touch in the Old Testament, with the book of Malachi, was in 165 B.C. by Judas Maccabeus, and it was closed to further edition until obviously the coming of the New Covenant with the coming of Christ. This was the canon. This was the officially accepted list of books, accepted by the Jewish leaders and the Jewish nation. [177]

OLD TESTAMENT AUTHORITY

Then of course Jesus enters the world and you read about his life and ministry in the four gospels. Jesus is consistently in conflict with the Jewish religious leaders because he poses such a threat to them. However, you do not see any record of any dispute between Jesus or his apostles over the books and the words contained in the Old Testament. You don't see Jesus come along and point out errors in the Old Testament.

Christ clearly had complete confidence in the text, and in the process confirmed the inspiration of scripture. One of the most compelling statements Jesus makes about the Old Testament record, is found early in the book of Matthew, when he says, "until heaven and earth pass away, not the smallest letter or stroke of the pen, will pass from God's Law." He is speaking of the permanence and everlasting truth found in the books of the Old Testament. (Matthew 5:18)

Jesus also regularly demonstrated his trust in the Old Testament using it as a reference when solving theological disputes with the Jewish leaders. In Mark 7:8-13, he refers to the entire Old Testament as "the commandment of God: and "the word of God." He clearly had a high and sacred view of these scriptures based upon the confidence he placed in them.

Roger Beckwith, an Old Testament scholar, who has written several books on the Old Testament canon, says,

> Sound historical studies show, therefore, that the Hebrew Old Testament, contains the true canon of the Old Testament shared by Jesus and the apostles with first century Judaism.[178]

NEW TESTAMENT AUTHORITY

What about the New Testament canon? If you look at Luke 24:48, John

15:27, and Acts 1:8, you see that Jesus makes it very clear that his apostles were to be designated witnesses and spokesmen out in the world after he was gone.

They were special men, and they had a special appointment, and you will notice in the four gospels that the twelve are referred to as his disciples. The word disciple means "a learner." In other words, what you had were these twelve men, and they were learning. They were being trained and equipped. They had been fishermen, tax collectors, and common lay people, and he was pouring his life into them, teaching them and instructing them. Later, Jesus appoints them as apostles, and then, of course, after Jesus' death, Judas kills himself and is replaced by Matthias. And you have Saul of Tarsus who also is appointed as an apostle. He becomes the apostle Paul and is clearly recognized by all the other apostles as being one of them. They approved it.

And this is what's so important to know: the word "apostle" means something completely different from "disciple." An "apostle" is a messenger. An emissary, a representative. They started out as students, as disciples, and then, he gave them the authority to be his representatives, his apostles out in the world. And he gave them a unique authority in the church. And this authority, this "apostleship," was not passed down. The apostles became agents of God's revelation, documenting what would become the Christian source of faith and life—the New Testament. And having been commissioned by Jesus, one of their primary assignments was clearly seen in John 14:26 and John 16:13-14.

These are Jesus' words, he says,

> But the Helper, the Holy Spirit, whom the Father will send in my name, he will teach you all things, and bring to your remembrance all that I said to you. (John 14:26)

> But when he, the Spirit of truth, comes, he will guide you into all the truth; for he will not speak on his own initiative, but whatever He hears, he will speak; and he will disclose to you what is to come.

> He will glorify Me, for he will take of Mine and will disclose it to you. (John 16:13, 14)

This is where we get our understanding of the inspiration of scripture, where God himself is involved with the process of leading and guiding the apostles in their writings. Peter reminds us that the words of scripture were not acts of human will, "but men moved by the Holy Spirit spoke from God." Therefore, in early church history, you see this pervasive recognition that the written words of the apostles were given full authority.

Consider the following words from the New Testament:

1. I John 4:6—John speaks of the Apostles "as being from God."

2. Johns opening words in the book of Revelation are "The revelation of Jesus Christ, which God gave him."

3. Paul speaks of the words in his letters as being taught by the spirit, expressing spiritual truths in spiritual words. (1 Corinthians 2:13)

4. In the same letter, Paul indicates that his writings "are the Lord's commands."

5. In Paul's opening words in the book of Galatians, he says:

> For I would have you know, brethren, that the gospel which was preached by me is not according to man.
>
> For I neither received it from man, nor was I taught it, but I received it through a revelation of Jesus Christ. (Galatians 1: 11,12)

6. In a letter to the church at Thessalonica, Paul says:

> For this reason we also constantly thank God that when you received the word of God which you heard from us, you accepted it not as the word of men, but for what it really is, the word of God, which also perform its work in you who believe. (1 Thessalonians 2:13)

You see in the early church father, Clement of Rome, a very distinguished, and very important church father, who died in 96 A.D., said,

> The apostles received the gospel for us from the Lord Jesus Christ. Jesus Christ was sent forth from God. So then, Christ is from God, and the apostles are from Christ. Both, therefore, came of the will of God in good order. [179]

And then, you see Clement cite verses from the New Testament in his writings. He cites from all gospels, the books of Acts, Romans, I Corinthians, Ephesians, Titus, Hebrews, and I Peter. Then the great philosopher, Justin

Martyr, who was born in 65 A.D. and died in 110 A.D., would in his writings quote often from the gospels, beginning his citations with these important words, *"It is written,"* which was his way of recognizing their scriptural authority. [180]

In the first century, the church and the church fathers regarded the gospels, Paul's letters, and Peter's letters, as authoritative scripture. And what you find is that at the end of the second century, there is this core collection of New Testament books that the Church regarded as scriptural authority. This original list of books entailed twenty-one of twenty-seven books that are in the current New Testament.

Dr. Winfried Cordman, a philosophy professor at Taylor University, says the early church had "a very straightforward project. They were collecting the writings of the apostles. The church recognized the former disciples, now apostles, were continuing the teachings of Jesus and were doing so with divine authority. He goes on to say, "The church also understood that this authority ended with the disciples."

It is important to point out that three of the books of the New Testament, Mark, Luke, and Acts, were not written by an Apostle. Mark apparently wrote the memoirs of Peter's teaching, and these memoirs were approved by Peter and therefore this apostolic association established Mark's account and inclusion in the canon.

Luke, the author of the book of Luke and Acts, was very close to Paul. In fact, Luke accompanied Paul, as an eyewitness on the missionary journeys you read about in last chapters of Acts.

For a number of years, there were questions about the books of James, II Peter, II and III John, Jude, and Revelation. Dr. Bruce Metzger of Princeton says,

> This indicates how very careful the early church fathers were in accepting a book into the New Testament canon. . . . It showed real deliberation and careful analysis during this process. [181]

Therefore, for many years, you had the twenty-one undisputed books of the New Testament and a couple of disputed books This lasted until the third century, when the church had three separate Synods, where key church leaders finally under the leadership of Augustine, agreed to the twenty-seven books of the New Testament that we have today. [182]

And what they finally concluded was that those six additional books were authentic and contained apostolic authority and therefore should be included in the New Testament canon. In the process, they excluded large numbers of books that people believed should be included in the canon. But they were highly selective, and what they really wanted to focus in on was which of these books are truly apostolic. This became the ultimate criterion, and this is how we have ended up with New Testament for both Protestant and Catholic believers.

As New Testament scholar Charles Hill says,

> The New Testament record remains as the permanent, documentary expression of God's new covenant. It may be said that only the twenty-seven books of the New Testament manifest themselves as belonging to that original, foundational, apostolic witness. They have demonstrated themselves to be the Word of God to the universal church throughout the generations. [183]

APPENDIX FOUR
ARCHEOLOGY

James Agresti, in his wonderful book, *Rational Conclusions*, documents the major archeological discoveries that corroborate so much of what is stated in the Bible, as far as people, places and events. In order to be included in the list, the archeological finds had to be compatible with the locations and approximate timing of such places, people, and events as described in the Bible.

Agresti identified almost 150 major archeological discoveries which authenticate the Biblical record. You will find below an abbreviated list, but they include those findings which are considered most significant.

For those who would prefer to skim this lengthy compilation, I have placed a star (*) in front of those I consider most significant. Also, in four places, I have placed two stars to highlight items I consider extraordinarily significant.

1. CITIES, TOWNS, EMPIRES AND LANDMARKS IN THE BIBLE CONFIRMED BY ARCHEOLOGICAL EVIDENCE.

*Cities of Ur and Haran (2,000-1,800 B.C)

Genesis 11:31: "And Terah took Abram his son, and Lot the son of Haran his son's son, and Sarai his daughter in law, his son Abram's wife; and they went forth with them from Ur of the Chaldees, to go into the land of Cannan; and they came unto Haran, and dwelt there."

*City of Hebron (17th century B.C.)

Genesis 37:14: "So he [Israel] sent him [Joseph] out of the vale of Hebron...."

*City of Hazor (13th century B.C.)

Joshua 11:10: "And Joshua at that time turned back, and took Hazor...."

City of Bethel (13th century B.C.)

Joshua 12:16 mentions "the king of Bethel."

*City of Gath (1,200-600 B.C.)

1 Samuel 17:4: "And there went out a champion out of the camp

of the Philistines, named Goliath, of Gath, whose height *was* six cubits and a span."

*City of Ashdod (12th-10th centuries B.C.)

1 Samuel 5:1: "And the Philistines took the ark of God, and brought it from Ebenezer unto Ashdod."

Kingdom of Assyria (9th-7th centuries B.C.)

2 Samuel 15:19 "*And* Pul the king of Assyria came against the land...."

*Babylonian Empire (6th century B.C.)

2 Kings 24:1: "in his days Nebuchadnezzar king of Babylon came up, and Jehoiakim became his servant three years: then he turned and rebelled against him."

*Town of Capernaum (1st century A.D.)

Matthew 8:5: "And when Jesus was entered into Capernaum, there came unto him a centurion, beseeching him...."

City of Caesarea Philippi (also known as Banias) (1st century A.D.)

Matthew 16:13: "When Jesus came into the coasts of Caesarea Philippi, he asked his disciples, saying, Whom do men say that I the Son of Man am?"

*City of Ephesus (1st century A.D.)

Acts 20:16: "For Paul had determined to sail by Ephesus...."

2. PEOPLE IN THE BIBLE CONFIRMED BY THE ARCHEOLOGICAL RECORD.

*The Philistines (12th century B.C.)

Judges 16:4-5: "And it came to pass afterward, that he [Samson] loved a woman in the valley of Sorek, whose name was Delilah. And the lords of the Philistines came up unto her..."

The Midianites (12th/11th centuries B.C.)

Judges 6:6: "And Israel was greatly impoverished because of the Midianites...."

*Ahab, king of Israel (9th century B.C.)

1 Kings 16:28: "So Omri slept with his fathers, and was buried in Samaria: and Ahab his son reigned in his stead."

Jeroboam II, king of Israel (8th century B.C.)

2 Kings 14:23: "In the fifteenth year of Amaziah the son of Joash king of Judah Jeroboam the son of Joash king of Israel began to reign in Samaria, *and reigned* forty and one years."

*Tiglath-pileser III, king of Assyria (8th century B.C.)

2 Kings 15:29: "In the days of Pekah king of Israel came Tiglath-Pileser king of Assyria, and took Ijon, and Abel-Beth-Maachah, and Janoah, and Kedesh, and Hazor, and Gilead, and Galilee, all the land of Naphtali, and carried them to captive Assyria."

*Hezekiah, king of Judah (8th/7th centuries B.C.)

2 Kings 16:20: "And Ahaz slept with his fathers, and was buried with his fathers in the city of David: and Hezekiah his son reigned in his stead."

Manasseh, king of Judah (7th century B.C.)

2 Kings 21:1: Manasseh *was* twelve years old when he began to reign, and reigned fifty and five years in Jerusalem."

*Gemariah, son of Shaphan (7th century B.C.)

Jeremiah 36:10: "Then read Baruch in the book the words of Jeremiah in the house of the LORD, in the chamber of Gemariah the son of Shaphan the scribe, in the higher court, at the entry of the new gate of the LORD'S house, in the ears of all the people."

*Belshazzar, effective ruler of Babylon (6th century B.C.)
Daniel 5:29: "Then commanded Belshazzar, and they clothed Daniel with scarlet, and *put* a chain of gold about his neck, and made a proclamation concerning him, that he should be the third ruler in the kingdom."

*Cyrus II, king of Persia (6th century B.C.)
Ezra 1:1: "Now in the first year of Cyrus king of Persia...."

*Darius the Great, king of Persia (6th/5th centuries B.C.)
Daniel 6:9: "Wherefore king Darius signed the writing and the decree."

Philip, son of Herod (1st century A.D.)
Luke 3:1: "[H] is brother Philip tetrarch of Ituraea and of the region of Trachonitis...."

*Erastus, city official in Corinth (1st century A.D.)
Romans 16:23: "Erastus the chamberlain of the city saluteth you...."

2 Timothy 4:20: "Erastus abode at Corinth...."

*Worship of a God named Asherah (also spelled Asherat) (13th century B.C.)
Deuteronomy 16:21 (NIV): "Do not set up any wooden Asherah pole beside the altar you build to the LORD your God...."

3. CUSTOMS AND PRACTICES IN THE BIBLE CONFIRMED BY ARCHEOLOGICAL EVIDENCE.

*Worship of a god named Baal (13th century B.C.)
Numbers 22:41: "And it came to pass on the morrow, that Balak took Balaam, and brought him up into high places of Baal, that thence he might see the utmost *part* of the people."

Judges 2:13: "And they forsook the LORD, and served Baal...."

*Babylonian practice of deporting the most skilled and learned citizens of a defeated enemy to Babylon and placing them in service of the Babylonian king (8th-6th centuries B.C.)

Daniel 1:1-4: "In the third year of the reign of Jehoiakim king of Judah came Nebuchadnezzar king of Babylon unto Jerusalem, and besieged it. And the Lord gave Jehoiakim king of Judah into his hand.... And the king spake unto Ashpenaz the master of his eunuchs, that he should bring *certain* of the children of Israel, and of the king's seed, and of the princes; Children in whom *was* no blemish, but well favoured, and skillful in all wisdom, and cunning in knowledge, and understanding science, and such as *had* ability in them to stand in the king's palace...."

**Rich people used tombs that were cut into bedrock. (1st century B.C.)

Matthew 27:57-60: "When the even was come, there came a rich man of Arimathaea, named Joseph, who also himself was Jesus' disciple: He went to Pilate, and begged the body of Jesus. Then Pilate commanded the body to be delivered. And when Joseph had taken the body, he wrapped it in a clean linen cloth, And laid it in his own new tomb, which he had hewn out in the rock: and he rolled a great stone to the door of the sepulcher, and departed."

*Shishak I (king of Egypt) attacked various place in Judea. (10th century B.C.)

1 Kings 14:25: "And it came to pass in the fifth year of king Rehoboam, *that* Shishak king of Egypt came up against Jerusalem: And he took away the treasures of the house of the LORD, and the treasures of the king's house; he even took way all: and he took away all the shields of gold which Solomon had made."

*Jehoram II (king of Israel) and Ahaziah II (king of Judah)

killed together (9th century B.C.)

2 Kings 9:24, 27: "And Jehu drew a bow with his full strength, and smote Jehoram between his arms, and the arrow went out at his heart, and he sunk down in his chariot.... But when Ahaziah the king of Judah saw *this*, he fled by the way of the garden house. And Jehu followed after him, and said, Smite him also in the chariot. *And they did so* at the going to Gur, which *is* by Ibleam. And he fled to Megiddo, and died there."

*Sargon II (king of Assyria) sent a high-ranking official to attack the city of Ashdod, and he defeated it. (8th century B.C.)

Isaiah 20:1: "In the year that Tartan [a high-ranking official] came unto Ashdod, (when Sargon the king of Assyria sent him,) and fought against Ashdod, and took it...."

*Sennacherib's troops surrounded Jerusalem, but no battle took place. (about 701 B.C.)

2 Kings 18:17; 19:35-36: "And the king of Assyria sent... a great host against Jerusalem. And it came to pass that night, that the angel of the LORD went out, and smote in the camp of the Assyrians an hundred fourscore and five thousand: and when they arose early in the morning, behold, they *were* all dead corpses. So Sennacherib king of Assyria departed, and went and returned, and dwelt at Nineveh."

*Hezekiah (king of Judah) constructed a conduit for the city's water supply. (about 701 B.C.)

2 Chronicles 32:30: "This same Hezekiah also stopped the upper watercourse of Gihon, and brought it straight down to the west side of the city of David."

2 Kings 20:20: "And the rest of the acts of Hezekiah, and all his might, and how he made a pool, and a conduit, and brought water into the city, *are* they not written in the book of the chronicles of the kings of Judah?"

*Nebuchadnezzar (king of Babylon) defeated Jehoiachin (king of Jerusalem), carried him off to Babylon, and appointed someone in his stead. (about 597 B.C.)

2 Kings 24:11, 15, 17: "And Nebuchadnezzar king of Babylon came against the city, and his servants did besiege it.... And he carried away Jehoiachin to Babylon, and the king's mother, and the king's wives, and his officers, and the mighty of the land, *those* carried he into captivity from Jerusalem to Babylon.... And the king of Babylon made Mattaniah his father's brother king in his stead, and changed his name to Zedekiah."

**While captive in Babylon, the sons of Jehoiakim (king of Judah) received an allowance from Nebuchadnezzar (king of the Babylonian Empire). (about 594 B.C.)

Daniel 1:1, 3, 5: "In the third year of the reign of Jehoiakim king of Judah came Nebuchadnezzar king of Babylon unto Jerusalem, and besieged it.... And the king spake unto Ashpenaz the master of his eunuchs, that he should bring *certain* of the children of Israel, and of the king's seed, and of the princes.... And the king appointed them a daily ration of the king's meat, and of the wine which he had drank." [184]

APPENDIX FIVE
HISTORY

Classical scholar and historian Colin Hemer chronicles Luke's accuracy in the book of Acts verse by verse. With painstaking detail, Hemer identifies eighty-four facts in the last sixteen chapters of Acts that have been confirmed by historical and archeological research. As you read the following list, keep in mind that Luke did not have access to modern-day maps or nautical charts. Luke accurately records—

1) the natural crossing between correctly named ports (So, being sent out by the Holy Spirit, they went down to Selecia and from there they sailed to Cyprus. When they reached Salamis, they begin to proclaim the word of God in the synagogues of the Jews; and they also had John as their helper. Acts 13:4-5)

2) the proper port (Perga) along the direct destination of a ship crossing from Cyprus (Now Paul and his companions put out to sea from Paphos and came to Perga in Pamphylia; but John left them and returned to Jerusalem. 13:13)

3) the proper location of Lycaonia (But going on from Perga they arrived at Pisidian Antioch, and on the Sabbath day they went into the synagogue and sat down. 14: 6)

4) the unusual but correct declension of the name Lystra (14:11)

5) the correct language spoken in Lystra—Lycaonian (14:11)

6) two gods known to be so associated—Zeus and Hermes (14:12)

7) the proper port, Attalia, which returning travelers would use (14:25)

8) the correct order of approach to Derbe and then to Lystra from the Cilcian Gates (16:1; cf. 15:41)

9) the proper form of the name Troas (16:8)

10) the place of a conspicuous sailors' landmark, Samothrace (16:11)

11) the proper description of Philippi as a Roman colony (16:12)

12) the right location for the river (Gangites) near Philippi (16:13)

13) the proper association of Thyatira as a center of dyeing (16:14)

14) correct designations for the magistrates of the colony (16:22)

15) the proper locations (Amphipolis and Apollonia) where travelers would spend successive nights on this journey (17:1)

16) the presence of a synagogue in Thessalonica (17:1)

17) the proper term ("politarchs") used of the magistrates there (17:6)

18) the correct implication that sea travel is the most convenient way of reaching Athens, with the favoring east winds of summer sailing (17:14-15)

19) the abundant presence of images in Athens. (17:16)

20) the reference to a synagogue in Athens (17:17)

21) the depiction of the Athenian life of philosophical debate in the Agora (17:17)

22) the use of the correct Athenian slang word for Paul (*spermologos*, 17:19) as well as for the court (*Areios pagos*, 17:19)

23) the proper characterization of the Athenian character (17:21)

24) an alter to an "unknown god" (17:23)

25) the proper reaction of Greek philosophers, who denied the bodily resurrection (17:32)

26) *Areopagites* as the correct title for a member of the court (17:34)

27) a Corinthian synagogue (18:4)

28) the correct designation of Gallio as proconsul, resident in Corinth (18:12)

29) the *bema* (judgment seat), which overlooks Corinth's forum (18:16ff.)

30) the name Tyrannus as attested from the Ephesus in first-century inscriptions (19:9)

31) well-known shrines and images of Artemis (19:24)

32) the well-attested "great goddess Artemis" (19:27)

33) that the Ephesian theatre was the meeting place of the city (19:29)

34) the correct title *grammateus* for the chief executive magistrate in Ephesus (19:35)

35) the proper title of honor *neokoros*, authorized by the Romans (19:35)

36) the correct name to designate the goddess (19:37)

37) the proper term for those holding court (19:38)

38) use of plural *anthupatoi*, perhaps a remarkable reference to the fact that *two* men were conjointly exercising the functions of proconsul at this time (19:38)

39) the "regular" assembly, as the precise phrase is attested elsewhere (19:39)

40) use of precise ethnic designation, *beroiaios* (20:4)

41) employment of the ethnic term *Asianos* (20:4)

42) the implied recognition of the strategic importance assigned to this city of Troas (20:7ff)

43) the danger of the coastal trip in this location (20:13)

44) the correct sequence of places (20:14-15)

45) the correct name of the city as a neuter plural (*Patara*) (21:1)

46) the appropriate route passing across the open sea south of Cyprus favored by persistent northwest winds (21:8)

47) the suitable distance between these cities (21:8)

48) a characteristically Jewish act of piety (21:24)

49) the Jewish law regarding Gentile use of the temple area (21:28) (Archaeological discoveries and quotations from Josephus confirm that Gentiles could be executed for entering the temple area. One inscription reads: "Let no Gentile enter within the balustrade and enclosure surrounding the sanctuary. Whoever is caught will be personally responsible for his consequent death.")

50) the permanent stationing of a Roman cohort (*chiliarch*) at Antonia to suppress any disturbance at festival times (21:31)

51) the flight of steps used by the guards (21:31, 35)

52) the common way to obtain Roman citizenship at this time (22:28)

53) the tribune being impressed with Roman rather than Tarsian citizenship (22:29)

54) Ananias being high priest at this time (23:2)

55) 55.Felix being governor at this time (23:34)

56) the natural stopping point on the way to Caesarea (23:31)

57) whose jurisdiction Cilicia was in at the time (23:34)

58) the provincial penal procedure of the time (24:1-9)

59) the name Porcius Festus, which agrees precisely with that given by Josephus (24:27)

60) the right of appeal for Roman citizens (25:11)

61) the correct legal formula (25:18)

62) the characteristic form of reference to the emperor at the time (25:26)

63) the best shipping lanes at the time (27:5)

64) the common bonding of Cilicia and Pamphylia (27:4)

65) the principle port to find a ship sailing to Italy (27:5-6)

66) the slow passage to Cnidus, in the face of the typical northwest winds (27:7)

67) the right route to sail, in view of the winds (27:7)

68) the locations of Fair Havens and the neighboring site of Lasea (27:8)

69) Fair Havens as a poorly sheltered roadstead (27:12)

70) a noted tendency of a south wind in these climes to back suddenly to a violent northeaster, the well-known *gregale* (27:13)

71) the nature of a square-rigged ancient ship, having no option but to be driven before a gale (27:15)

72) the precise place and name of this island (27:16)

73) the appropriate maneuvers for the safety of the ship in its particular plight (27:16)

74) the fourteenth night—a remarkable calculation, based inevitably on a compounding of estimates and probabilities, confirmed in the judgment of experienced Mediterranean navigators (27:27)

75) the proper term of the time for the Adriatic (27:27)

76) the precise term (*Bolisantes*) for taking soundings, and the correct depth of the water near Malta (27:28)

77) a position that suits the probable line of approach of a ship released to run before an easterly wind (27:39)

78) the severe liability on guards who permitted a prisoner to escape (27:42)

79) the local people and superstitions of the day (28:4-6)

80) the proper title *protos tēs nēsou* (28:7)

81) Rhegium as a refuge to await a southerly wind to carry them through the strait (28:13)

82) Appii Forum and Tres Tabernae as correctly placed stopping places on the Appian Way (28:15)

83) appropriate means of custody with Roman soldiers (28:16)

84) the conditions of imprisonment, living "at his own expense" (28:30-31) [185]

CHAPTER NOTES

1. Nicholi, Armand, *The Question of God*, Free Press, A Division of Simon & Schuster, 2002, p. 83, 84.
2. Nicholi, Armand, Ibid., p. 86.
3. Nicholi, Armand, Ibid., p. 87.
4. Keller, Timothy, *The Reason for God*, Penguin Group, 2008, p. 99.
5. Simmons, Richard, *Remembering the Forgotten God*, 1993, p. 55.
6. Nicholi, *The Question of God*, op. cit., p. 85.
7. Grenz, Stanley J., Guretzki, David, & Nordling, Cherith Fee, *Pocket Dictionary of Theological Terms*, Intervarsity Press, 2999, p. 52.
8. Sartre, Jean-Paul & Levy, Benny, Translated by Van Den Hoven, Adrian, *Hope Now: The 1980 Interviews*, The University of Chicago Press, 1996, p110.
9. Stanford, Miles, *The Complete Green Letters*, Zondervan, 1983, p. 3.
10. Montgomery, John Warwick, *History and Christianity*, Bethany House Publishers, 1973, p. 15, 16.
11. Carlson, Ron, and Carlson, Jason, Essay: "Is the Bible the Inspired Word of God?" May 25, 2011.
12. Yancey, Philip, *The Bible Jesus Read*, Zondervan, 1999, p. 21.
13. Cailliet, Emile, *Journey Into Light*, Zondervan, 1968, p. 16.
14. Cailliet, Emile, Ibid., p. 18.
15. Kullberg, Kelly Monroe, *Finding God Beyond Harvard*, Intervarsity Press, 2006, p. 138, 139.
16. Zacharias, Ravi, Essay from *A Slice of Infinity*, "Word and Culture," November 16, 2006.
17. Collins, Francis, *A Place for Truth*, Intervarsity Press, 2010, p. 77.
18. Collins, Francis, *Mere Christians*, Baker Books, 2009, p. 79
19. Carattini, Jill, Essay from *A Slice of Infinity*, "A Reasonable Faith," October 26, 2006.
20. Smith, Huston, *The World's Religions*, Harper, San Francisco, 1961, p. 317.
21. Zacharias, Ravi, Essay from *A Slice of Infinity*, "Christianity Without Christ," February 1, 2012.
22. Lindsley, Dr. Arthur, Essay from the C.S. Lewis Institute, "Can The Gospels Be

Trusted?" May 25, 2012.

23. Strobel, Lee, *The Case for Christ*, Zondervan, 1998, p. 45.
24. Keller, Timothy, Sermon, Redeemer Presbyterian Church, "Come and See," November 15, 1998.
25. Keller, Timothy, Ibid.
26. Geisler, Norman, and Turek, Frank, *I Don't Have Enough Faith To Be An Atheist*, Crossway Books, 2004, p. 275.
27. Strobel, Lee, *The Case for Christ*, op. cit., p. 86.
28. Ibid., p. 51.
29. Agresti, James D., *Rational Conclusions*, Documentary Press, 2009, p. 29.
30. Orr-Ewing, Amy, *Why Trust the Bible*, Intervarsity Press, 2005, p. 59.
31. Strobel, Lee, *The Case for Christ*, op. cit., p. 79, 80.
32. Ibid., p. 79, 80.
33. Geisler, *I Don't Have Enough Faith to be an Atheist*, op. cit., p. 223.
34. Strobel, Lee, *The Case for Christ*, op. cit., p. 89.
35. Geisler, *I Don't Have Enough Faith to be an Atheist*, op. cit., p. 227, 228.
36. Ibid., 256.
37. Geisler, *I Don't Have Enough Faith to be an Atheist*, op. cit., p. 260.
38. McDowell, Josh, *Evidence that Demands a Verdict*, Here's Life Publishers, 1972, p. 71.
39. Kennedy, D. James, *Why I Believe*, Word Publishing, 1980, p. 33.
40. Yancey, Philip, *Disappointment with God*, Zondervan, 1988, p. 47, 48.
41. Price, Randall, *The Stones Cry Out*, Harvest House Publishers, 1997, p. 21.
42. Strobel, Lee, *The Case for Christ*, op. cit., p. 96.
43. Sheler, Jeffery, *Is The Bible True?* Harper Collins, 1999, p. 73 – 75.
44. Maugh II, Thomas H., "Biblical Pool Uncovered in Jerusalem," *The Los Angeles Times*, September 8, 2005.
45. Price, *The Stones Cry Out*, op. cit., p 82, 83.
46. Boice, James Montgomery, *An Expositional Commentary: Acts*, Baker Books, 1997, p. 290.
47. Strobel, Lee, *The Case for Christ*, op. cit., p. 107.
48. Strobel, Lee, *The Case for Christ*, op. cit., p. 107.
49. Sheler, *Is the Bible True?* op. cit., p. 156.
50. Sheler, *Is the Bible True?* op. cit., p. 156.
51. Sheler, *Is the Bible True?* op. cit., p. 156.
52. Sheler, Jeffery, *U.S. News and World Report*, "Mysteries of the Bible," April 17, 1995, p. 60, 61.
53. Sheler, *Is the Bible True?* op. cit., p. 157.
54. Strobel, Lee, *The Case for Christ*, op. cit., p. 94.
55. Sheler, *Is the Bible True?* op. cit., p. 156.
56. McDowell, *Evidence That Demands a Verdict*, op. cit., p. 65.
57. Agresti, *Rational Conclusions*, op. cit., p. 88.
58. McDowell, *Evidence That Demands a Verdict*, op. cit., p. 65.
59. Agresti, *Rational Conclusions*, op. cit., p. 88.
60. Zacharias, Ravi, Presentation: "Asked and Answered," 2006.
61. Zacharias, Ravi, Essay from A Slice of Infinity, "Word and Culture," November

16, 2006.

62. Agresti, *Rational Conclusions*, op. cit.

63. Carattini, Jill, Essay from Slice of Infinity, "A Voice Recognized," August 8, 2005.

64. Agresti, *Rational Conclusions*, op. cit., p. 15, 16.

65. McDowell, *Evidence that Demands a Verdict*, op. cit., p. 42.

66. Orr-Ewing, *Why Trust the Bible?* op. cit.

67. Agresti, *Rational Conclusions*, op. cit., p. 129.

68. Strobel, Lee, *The Case for Christ*, op. cit., p. 59.

69. Agresti, *Rational Conclusions*, op. cit., p. 129.

70. Geisler, *I Don't Have Enough Faith To Be An Atheist*, op. cit., p. 225.

71. McDowell, *Evidence that Demands a Verdict*, op. cit., p. 42.

72. Orr-Ewing, *Why Trust the Bible?* op. cit., p. 41.

73. Orr-Ewing, *Why Trust the Bible?* op. cit., p. 41.

74. Geisler, *I Don't Have Enough Faith To Be An Atheist*, op. cit., p. 237, 238.

75. Orr-Ewing, *Why Trust the Bible?* op. cit., p. 40.

76. Geisler, *I Don't Have Enough Faith To Be An Atheist*, op. cit., p. 227.

77. Orr-Ewing, *Why Trust the Bible?* op. cit., p. 39.

78. Strobel, Lee, *The Case for Christ*, op. cit., p. 70.

79. Montgomery, *History and Christianity*, op. cit., p. 28.

80. Habermas, Gary, *Why I Am A Christian*, from the essay "Why I Believe the New Testament is Historically Reliable," Baker Books, 2003, p. 148 – 149.

81. Orr-Ewing, *Why Trust the Bible?* p. 42.

82. Sheler, *Is the Bible True?* op. cit., p. 168.

83. Sheler, *Is the Bible True?* op. cit., p. 169

84. Sheler, *Is the Bible True?* op. cit., p. 196.

85. Sheler, *Is the Bible True?* op. cit., p. 197.

86. McDowell, *Evidence that Demands a Verdict*, op. cit., p. 58.

87. Agresti, *Rational Conclusions*, op. cit., p. 124.

88. McDowell, *Evidence that Demands a Verdict*, op. cit., p. 19.

89. Strobel, Lee, *The Case for Christ*, op. cit., p. 14.

90. Strobel, Lee, *The Case for Christ*, op. cit., p. 57, 58.

91. Strobel, Lee, *The Case for Christ*, op. cit., p. 71.

92. Manning, Margaret, Essay in Slice of Infinity, "The Great False Dichotomy," August 25, 2009.

93. Zacharias, Ravi, *The End of Reason*, Zondervan, 2008, p. 105.

94. Collins, Francis, "The Language of God," from *A Place for Truth*, Intervarsity Press, p. 89.

95. Collins, Francis, "The Language of God," ibid., p. 89.

96. Guillen, Dr. Michael, *Can a Smart Person Believe in God*, Nelson Books, 2004, p. 75.

97. McGrath, Dr. Alister, "The New Atheists and the Meaning of Life," from *A Place for Truth*, p. 102.

98. Strobel, Lee, *The Case for a Creator*, op. cit., p. 74, 75.

99. Strobel, Lee, *The Case for a Creator*, op. cit., p. 74.

100. Strobel, Lee, *The Case for a Creator*, op. cit., p. 69 – 71.

101. Agresti, *Rational Conclusions*, op. cit., p. 47.
102. Agresti, *Rational Conclusions*, op. cit., p. 51.
103. Flew, Anthony, *There is a God*, Harper One, 2007, p. 88.
104. Keller, *Reason for God*, op. cit., p. 130.
105. Masci, David, Senior Researcher, The Pew Forum, "Scientists Not Entirely Without Belief in God" from *The Los Angeles Times* and in *The Birmingham News*, November 27, 2009.
106. Geisler, *I Don't Have Enough Faith to Be An Atheist*, op. cit., p. 73, 74.
107. Geisler, *I Don't Have Enough Faith to Be An Atheist*, op. cit., p. 74.
108. Strobel, Lee, *The Case for a Creator*, op. cit., p. 70.
109. Strobel, Lee, *The Case for a Creator*, op. cit., p. 77.
110. Strobel, Lee, *The Case for a Creator*, op. cit., p. 77.
111. Strobel, Lee, *The Case for a Creator*, op. cit., p. 19, 37, 38.
112. Strobel, Lee, *The Case for Faith*, op. cit., p. 96.
113. Strobel, Lee, *The Case for Faith*, op. cit., p. 97.
114. Strobel, Lee, *The Case for Faith*, p. 107,108.
115. Geisler, *I Don't Have Enough Faith to Be An Atheist*, op. cit., p. 121.
116. Geisler, *I Don't Have Enough Faith to Be An Atheist*, op. cit., p. 121.
117. Strobel, Lee, *The Case for Faith*, op. cit., p. 100.
118. Strobel, Lee, *The Case for Faith*, op. cit., p. 140.
119. Lennox, John, from a presentation made in conjunction with the Ravi Zacharias International Ministries, "The Word of God in Creation," 2011.
120. Agresti, *Rational Conclusions*, op. cit., p. 289.
121. Strobel, Lee, *The Case for Faith*, op. cit., p. 91.
122. Agresti, *Rational Conclusions*, op. cit., p. 260.
123. Agresti, *Rational Conclusions*, op. cit., p. 289.
124. Agresti, *Rational Conclusions*, op. cit., p. 289.
125. Strobel, Lee, *The Case for a Creator*, op. cit., p. 61, 62.
126. Strobel, Lee, *The Case for a Creator*, op. cit., p. 62.
127. Switek, Brian, "Bones That Tell a Tale," *The Wall Street Journal*, October 8, 2011, p. C6.
128. From the Population Reference Bureau, as of 2011.
129. Strobel, Lee, *The Case for Faith*, op. cit., p. 111.
130. Brooks, David, "If It Feels Right," *The New York Times*, September 12, 2011.
131. Miller, Donald, *Blue Like Jazz*, Thomas Nelson, 2003, p. 22.
132. Lewis, C.S., *Mere Christianity*, Macmillan Publishing Co, Inc., 1981, p. 6.
133. De Demarco, Donald, *Architects of the Culture of Death*, Ignatius Press, 2004, p. 29.
134. Kreeft, Peter, *C. S. Lewis for the Third Millennium*, Ignatius Press, 1004, p. 43, 44.
135. Colson, Charles, *Kingdoms in Conflict*, Zondervan Publishing, 1987, p. 71.
136. Simmons, III, Richard E., *Remembering the Forgotten God*, op. cit., p. 19.
137. Moreland, J.P., presentation at Rice University at a Veritas Forum.
138. Montgomery, John Warwick, *A Place for Truth*, Chapter 13, "Why Human Rights Are Impossible Without Religion," p. 264.
139. Simmons, III, Richard E., *Remembering the Forgotten God*, op. cit., p. 138.

140. Keller, Tim, Sermon at Redeemer Presbyterian, "Wisdom: Strangeness and The Order of God," October 30, 2004.

141. Taunton, Larry, *The Grace Effect*, Thomas Nelson, 2011, p. 1.

142. Schmidt, Alvin, *How Christianity Changed the World*, Zondervan, 2004, p. 48, 122, 147, 166, 289.

143. Nicholi, *The Question of God*, op. cit., p. 113.

144. Geisler, Norman, *Intellectuals Speak Out About God*, Regency Gateway 1984, p. 147, 148.

145. Kreeft, *C. S. Lewis for the 3rd Millennium*, op. cit., p. 91.

146. Kreeft, *C. S. Lewis for the 3rd Millennium*, op. cit., p. 91.

147. Pearcey, Nancy R., *Total Truth*, Crossway Books, 2004, p. 60, 61.

148. Yancey, Philip, *Soul Survivor*, Doubleday, 2001, p. 115, 116.

149. Keller, Timothy, *The Reason for God*, op. cit., p. 229, 230.

150. Lewis, *Mere Christianity*, op. cit., p. 45.

151. Lewis, C. S., *The Grand Miracle*, Ballantine Books, 1986, p. 113.

152. Lewis, C. S., *The Grand Miracle*, ibid., p. 114.

153. Yancey, Philip, *The Jesus I Never Knew*, Zondervan Publishing House, 1995, p. 17.

154. Yancey, Philip, *The Jesus I Never Knew*, ibid., p. 17.

155. Montgomery, J. W., *History & Christianity*, op. cit., p. 62.

156. Bosch, Henry, *Encyclopedia of 7,700 Illustrations*, Assurance Publishers, 1985, p. 647.

157. Yancey, Philip, *The Jesus I Never Knew*, as cited in Durant, Will, infra, The Story of Civilization.

158. Durant, Will, *The Story of Civilization: Caesar and Christ—A History of Roman Civilization and Christianity from their beginnings to A.D. 325 through 557.*

159. Yancey, Philip, *The Bible Jesus Read*, op. cit., p. 24.

160. Kreeft, Peter, *Christianity for Modern Pagans*, Ignatius Press, 1966, p. 263.

161. Ibid., p. 264.

162. Geisler, *I Don't Have Enough Faith to Be An Atheist*, op. cit., p. 327–329, 332, 337–338.

163. Keller, Timothy, *King's Cross*, Dutton/Penguin Group, 2011, p. 154.

164. Strobel, Lee, *The Case for Christ*, op. cit., p. 172–181.

165. Morison, Frank, *Who Moved the Stone*, Zondervan 1930.

166. Habermas, Gary R., as cited in Geisler, Norman, *I Don't Have Enough Faith to Be An Atheist*, op. cit., p. 299-300.

167. *U.S News and World Report*, "The Last Days of Jesus," April 16, 1990, p. 53.

168. McDowell, *Evidence that Demands a Verdict*, op. cit., p. 190 – 191.

169. Anders, Max, *Holman Old Testament Commentary*, "Ecclesiastes: Song of Solomon," 2003, p. 4.

170. Zacharias, Ravi, *Jesus Among Other Gods*, Word Publishing, 2000, p. 150.

171. Yancey, Philip, *What Good is God*, FaithWords, 2010, p. 215 – 216.

172. Vanauken, Sheldon, *A Severe Mercy*, Harper One, 1977, p. 98, 99.

173. Stott, John, *Through the Bible*, Baker Books, 2006, p. 109

174. Stott, John, ibid., p. 398

175. Beckwith, Roger, *Understanding Scripture*, Crossway, 2012, p. 78